OCEANS ATLAS

Author

John Woodward

Consultant

Professor Dorrik Stow

DK

LONDON, NEW YORK,
MELBOURNE, MUNICH, AND DELHI

Project art editor Philip Letsu
Designer Sheila Collins
Senior editor Shaila Brown
Editors Jenny Finch, Fran Baines
Managing editor Linda Esposito
Managing art editor Diane Thistlethwaite
Publishing manager Andrew Macintyre
Category publisher Laura Buller
Picture researcher Jo Walton and Julia Harris-Voss
DK picture library Sarah Stewart-Richardson
Production controller Angela Graef
DTP designer Siu Chan
Jacket editor Mariza O'Keeffe
Jacket designer Johnny Pau
Jacket manager Sophia M. Tampakopoulos Turner
Illustrators Andrew Kerr, Lee Gibbons
Cartographer Ed Merritt
CD-Rom project manager Anthony Pearson

First American Edition, 2007
Published in the United States by
DK Publishing, 375 Hudson Street, New York, New York, 10014

10 11 10 9 8 7 6 5 4

Copyright © 2007 Dorling Kindersley Limited
All rights reserved under Pan-American and International Copyright
Conventions. No part of this publication may be reproduced,
stored in a retrieval system, or transmitted in any form or by any means,
electronic, mechanical, photocopying, recording, or otherwise, without
the prior written permission of the copyright owner. Published in Great
Britain by Dorling Kindersley Limited.

A catalog record for this book is available from the Library of Congress.

ISBN: 978-0-7566-2557-3

Color reproduction by Colourscan, Singapore
Printed by Hung Hing, China

Discover more at
www.dk.com

How to run Oceans Atlas CD-ROM
Windows® PC
Insert the disk into your computer's CD-ROM drive.
The program will start automatically.

Apple Macintosh®
Insert the disk into your computer's CD-ROM drive. Double click
on the Oceans Atlas CD-ROM icon to open the CD window.
To run the program in OSX, click on the OSX icon.
To run the program in OS9, click on the Mac icon.

Minimum system requirements
Windows® PC
Intel Pentium® II 300MHz (Intel Pentium®III 1GHz
or higher recommended)
Windows® 98SE, 2000, ME, XP
64Mb RAM (256Mb RAM or higher recommended)
800 x 600 16-bit colour (32-bit colour recommended)
8-speed CD-ROM drive (24-speed CD-ROM drive recommended)

Power Macintosh Power PC processor G3 (G4 or higher recommended)
Mac® OS 9.2, OSX
64MB RAM (256Mb RAM or higher recommended)
800 x 600 16-bit colour (32-bit colour recommended)
8-speed CD-ROM drive (24-speed CD-ROM drive recommended)

Contents

Oceans and Continents 4
Moving Plates 6
Ocean Water 8
Ocean Currents 10
Tides 12
Wind and Wave 14
Cliffs and Beaches 16
Oceanic Gardens 18
Life in Sunlit Oceans 20
Life in the Dark 22

ARCTIC OCEAN **24**
Polar Ice Sheet 26
Siberian Seas 28
Canadian Arctic 30

ATLANTIC OCEAN **32**
Northwest Atlantic 34
Mid-Atlantic Ridge 36
Northeast Atlantic 38
Mediterranean and Black Sea 40
Tropical North Atlantic 42
Caribbean 44
Gulf of Mexico 46
West African Seas 48

INDIAN OCEAN **50**
Mozambique Channel 52
Arabian Seas 54
Bay of Bengal 56
The Sunda Arc 58

PACIFIC OCEAN **60**
China Seas 62
Great Barrier Reef 64
Oceania 66
Hawaii 68
Gulf of Alaska 70
East Pacific Rise 72
The Galápagos 74

SOUTHERN OCEAN **76**
Subantarctic Islands 78
Weddell Sea 80
The Icy Ocean 82

OCEAN FACTS **84**
Ocean Pioneers 86
Scientific Exploration 88
Exploiting the Oceans 90
Ocean Conservation 92
Glossary 94
Index 96

Oceans and Continents

THE OCEANS ARE VAST. They cover more than two-thirds of the planet and have a total volume of about 319 million cubic miles (1,330 million cubic km)—more than ten times the volume of land above sea level. But they are not just huge pools of water. The ocean floors are areas where the Earth's deep, hot interior has just a thin crust of dark, heavy rock. This thin oceanic crust surrounds much thicker slabs of lighter rock that form the continents and beds of shallow coastal seas.

CONTINENTAL SLOPE

CONTINENTAL SHELF

CONTINENTAL CRUST

LAYER OF SEDIMENT

OCEANIC CRUST

MANTLE

▲ FLOATING CONTINENTS

The relatively light rocks that make up continents float on the Earth's dense mantle rock like rafts on water. Below them float the harder, heavier rocks that make up the ocean crust. Water has filled the low-lying gaps between continents to create the oceans.

MOLTEN BASALT LAVA boils up from a volcanic vent in Hawaii, in the central Pacific

BLUE PLANET ▶

The Pacific Ocean alone covers nearly half the globe. If you could view the Earth from a position in space directly above the South Pacific you would see a largely blue planet, with only a few scattered fragments of land. The oceans are where life on Earth began and are what makes our planet unique.

LIQUID LAVA cools and solidifies into black basalt— the same rock that forms the ocean floors

◀ BASALT FLOORS

Ocean floors are made from various forms of basalt—a dark, dense rock that erupts from oceanic volcanoes as very fluid lava. Continents are made of lighter rocks, such as granite, which float higher on the very dense rock of the mantle.

CONTINENTAL SHELVES ▶

The fringes of continents extend underwater as shallow continental shelves. So the true edge of a continent lies at the limit of its shelf, at the continental slope where the water depth increases dramatically to the depths of the ocean. This 3-D map of the sea floor off California shows the shelf region in orange, and the continental slope in yellow, green, and pale blue.

MICROSCOPIC SKELETONS of marine organisms form thick sediments.

◀ SEABED SEDIMENTS

The hard bedrocks of the continental shelves and ocean floors are covered with softer sediments. Some of these are carried off the land by rivers, but others settle out of the water. They include the mineral skeletons of microscopic living things. As layer upon layer of sediments build up they are gradually compressed into solid rock.

ROCK LAYERS were laid down as soft sediments beneath oceans

SEDIMENTARY ROCKS ▶

The sediments that settle on ocean floors start off as layers of soft mud and sand, but are compressed to form sedimentary rocks. In many places, ground movements have raised these rocks above sea level, where they have been cut away by erosion to reveal the various layers. These often contain fossils of sea creatures, and since the oldest layers nearly always lie beneath more recent ones, they can reveal how marine life has evolved over time.

THE OCEANS have an average depth of more than 2 miles (3.5 km)

Moving Plates

THE OCEANS ARE NOT FIXED IN SIZE OR SHAPE. They change as the rigid plates of the Earth's crust slip apart or push together. The plates move apart at midocean ridges, where molten rock erupts from spreading rifts in the ocean floor. Other plate boundaries are subduction zones where one plate is diving beneath another, creating ocean trenches, earthquakes, chains of volcanoes, and mountain ridges on continental margins. Although the continents are pushed around the globe by these movements, they survive intact. The ocean floor, however, is continually being created and destroyed.

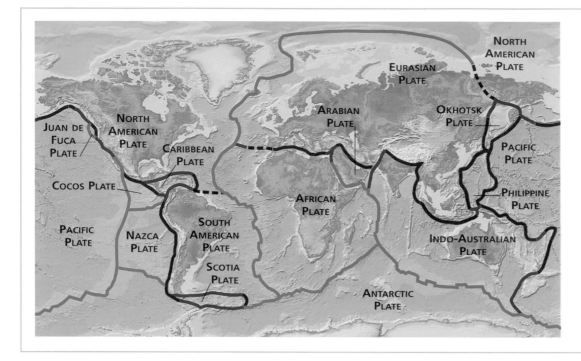

◄ FRACTURED EARTH

The brittle crust of the Earth is divided into separate plates, which are pushed around by currents in the hot mantle rock below. They are drawn together at convergent boundaries marked by ocean trenches and volcanic earthquake zones, and dragged apart at divergent midocean ridges. Some of the plates are entirely oceanic, but others carry continents very slowly around the globe.

———————	CONVERGENT BOUNDARY
———————	DIVERGENT BOUNDARY
———————	SLIDING BOUNDARY
– – – –	UNCERTAIN BOUNDARY

SPREADING RIDGES ►

Ocean crust is created at a divergent plate boundary where the plates are being pulled apart. As the rift opens it relieves the pressure on the hot mantle rock below, making it melt and squirt up through fissures like red-hot toothpaste. The molten rock soon solidifies in the cold ocean water, creating a tumbled mass of "pillow lava" that is slowly drawn away from the rift, allowing more molten rock to erupt from below.

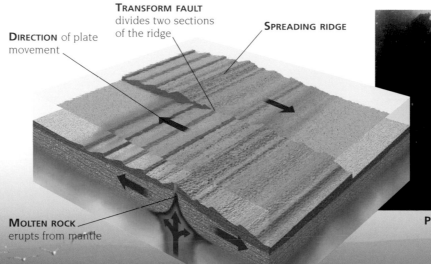

TRANSFORM FAULT divides two sections of the ridge

DIRECTION of plate movement

SPREADING RIDGE

MOLTEN ROCK erupts from mantle

PILLOW LAVA FORMING DEEP BELOW THE PACIFIC

VOLCANIC ISLAND ARC

MOLTEN ROCK forced up

PLATE dragged under

◀ SUBDUCTION ZONES

In places where the ocean crust is being subducted, or dragged beneath the edges of neighboring plates, it forms long, deep trenches in the ocean floor. As the sinking crust plunges downward, it triggers earthquakes and creates lines of submarine volcanoes that erupt through the plate margin above. These eventually become volcanic island arcs like the Aleutian Islands off Alaska, shown above.

TRENCHES AND SHELVES ▶

Where continents border on subduction zones they have narrow continental shelves that plunge into deep ocean trenches, and the land is pushed up into mountains. Coasts that are not affected by subduction are usually low-lying, with broad continental shelves.

DEEP OCEAN TRENCH

SUBDUCTION on the Pacific side of South America has created a deep trench

PASSIVE BOUNDARY with the Atlantic has a broad continental shelf

▼ MOVING CONTINENTS

The creation and destruction of ocean floor drags the continents around the globe, shuffling them into new combinations. They move extremely slowly, at about the rate that our fingernails grow, but over millions of years this can reshape the world.

200 MILLION YEARS AGO, continents were locked together in a supercontinent called Pangaea, surrounded by a global ocean

100 MILLION YEARS LATER, Pangaea was splitting apart, and the Atlantic was opening up between America and Africa

TODAY, India has crashed into Asia, and Australia is moving north. The Atlantic is still growing, but the Pacific is shrinking

▼ NEW OCEANS

Spreading rifts that pass through continents may develop into open oceans in the future. The Great Rift Valley of east Africa links up with the Red Sea rift and has already broadened into deep lakes that are home to thousands of flamingos.

Ocean Water

OCEAN BASINS ARE FILLED WITH WATER, which has some unusual properties. On Earth it can exist in three forms at once—as solid ice, liquid water, and water vapor, which is a gas. This enables water to occur on the Earth's surface and form part of the atmosphere. As it changes from one form to another water releases or absorbs energy, causing heating and cooling that help drive the world's weather systems. These carry water around the globe, and from the oceans to the land, as clouds and rain. The rain that falls on land eventually flows back to the oceans in rivers, carrying dissolved minerals that are essential to marine life. Most life is found near the ocean surface, because the sunlight it needs to survive is soon absorbed by the water and cannot penetrate the depths.

▲ VOLCANIC ORIGINS

Ocean water probably originated as water vapor and other gases that erupted from huge volcanoes early in the history of the Earth. The gases condensed into clouds that poured chemically rich rain onto the Earth's surface. Over millions of years this accumulated into vast oceans that may once have covered most of the planet.

COMET HALE-BOPP came close to Earth in 1997

RAIN falls as clouds rise over high land and cool

WATER VAPOR rises from lakes

CLOUDS blow over land

SNOW falls on mountain peaks

COOLED WATER VAPOR forms clouds

PLANTS produce more water vapor

WATER drains off the land in streams and rivers

WARM WATER VAPOR rises into the air

GROUND WATER seeps into the rock

◄ WATER CYCLE

The Sun's heat makes water evaporate from the oceans, forming clouds that may be carried over land. Here they spill rain that seeps through the ground and flows back to the sea. This "fresh water" contains minerals dissolved from rocks, the organic remains of living things, and dissolved oxygen, carbon dioxide, and other gases.

▲ WATER FROM SPACE

Comets are largely made of ice, and some ocean water may have originated from comet impacts early in the planet's history. This "extraterrestrial water" may have also contained the complex molecules that formed the seeds of life on Earth.

◄ SALTY SEAWATER

When water turns to water vapor any dissolved impurities are left behind, just like the salt crystals on this salt lake shore. Over billions of years, erosion and dissolution of rocks on land has carried chemical salts to the sea. The sea tastes salty because the main chemical ingredient is sodium chloride, or common salt. But the water also contains other substances that are vital nutrients for marine life.

WATER returns to the sea

◄ DENSITY AND PRESSURE

Water, with its high salt content, is relatively dense, which is why things that are not so dense—like logs, rafts, and even people—float on it. This enables sea animals such as whales to grow to enormous sizes, since they do not have to support their own weight. The weight of the water creates such high pressures at depth that deep diving by humans is impossible without pressure-proof submersibles.

LIGHT ZONES ▶

Ocean water reflects a lot of light, so it is always darker below the ocean surface. But water also absorbs light. White sunlight is made of all the colors of the rainbow, and the water of the sunlit zone absorbs the different colors at different rates. Red is absorbed first, then orange, yellow, green, and violet. Eventually there is only dim blue light left, creating the twilight zone. Finally even the blue light is absorbed, and the twilight gives way to the dark zone.

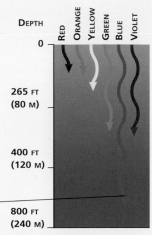

DEPTH	RED	ORANGE	YELLOW	GREEN	BLUE	VIOLET
0						
265 FT (80 M)						
400 FT (120 M)						
800 FT (240 M)						

BLUE LIGHT penetrates much deeper than the other colors that make up white sunlight, creating the deep twilight zone

WHITE LIGHT from a camera flashlight shows the true colors of a coral reef, just as they would appear in white sunlight that is not filtered by the water.

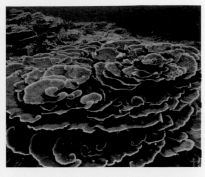

WITHOUT FLASH the deeper parts of the reef look blue, because the sunlight filtering down to the coral has been stripped of its red and yellow light.

Ocean Currents

OCEAN WATER IS ALWAYS MOVING, but some water masses move a lot more than others. These "rivers" of ocean water are known as currents. They are driven by the wind at the surface and by changes of temperature and saltiness that increase the density of water, making it heavier so it sinks and flows along the ocean floor. The surface and deep-water currents are all linked in an oceanic conveyor belt that slowly carries ocean water around the globe, redistributing heat from the tropics to the polar regions.

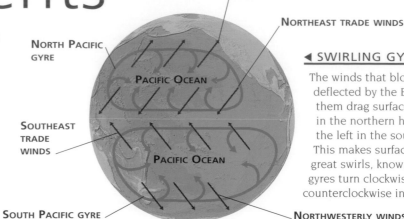

SOUTHWESTERLY WINDS

NORTHEAST TRADE WINDS

NORTH PACIFIC GYRE

PACIFIC OCEAN

SOUTHEAST TRADE WINDS

PACIFIC OCEAN

SOUTH PACIFIC GYRE

NORTHWESTERLY WINDS

◀ SWIRLING GYRES

The winds that blow over oceans are deflected by the Earth's spin, making them drag surface water to the right in the northern hemisphere and to the left in the southern hemisphere. This makes surface currents turn in great swirls, known as gyres. The gyres turn clockwise in the north and counterclockwise in the south.

SURFACE CURRENTS ▶

Prevailing winds tend to make surface currents swirl around the oceans in large gyres. But the current pattern is complicated by the shapes of the continents, local winds, and seasonal wind changes caused by continents heating up and cooling down. At the equator, light winds allow ocean water pushed west by current gyres to flow back east in equatorial countercurrents.

→ WARM OCEAN CURRENTS

→ COLD OCEAN CURRENTS

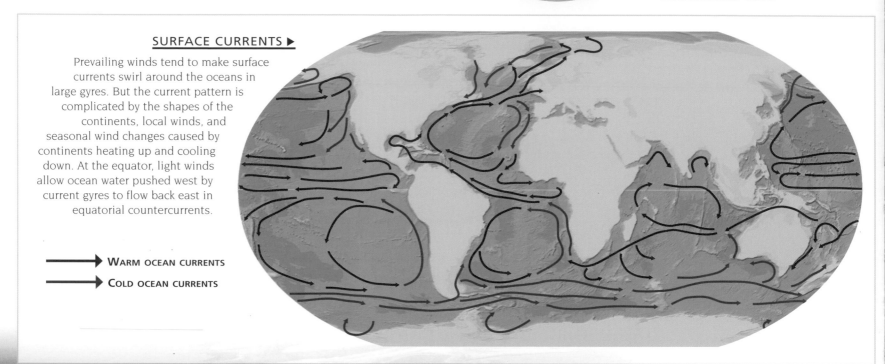

◀ OCEANIC ANIMALS

Many oceanic animals instinctively make use of surface currents to help them make long journeys with relatively little effort. Riding the currents enables the leatherback sea turtle to cross oceans, as it migrates between its tropical breeding beaches and the cooler seas where it finds a lot of its jellyfish prey.

LONG FLIPPERS enable the turtle to swim slowly, but it relies on currents to carry it across oceans

DEEP CHILL ▶

Water becomes denser if it gets colder or more salty, so becomes heavier and sinks. This helps drive what is known as thermohaline circulation, the force that powers the movement of deep-water currents. The most powerful "engines" are icebound polar seas, where ice forming at the surface expels salt into the water below, as well as cooling it. The cold, extra-salty water sinks and flows away near the ocean floor, creating a deep-water current.

SURFACE WATER flows in to replace the water that is sinking

SALT is expelled from sea water as it freezes

FLOATING ICE chills the water below and makes more ice form

COLD, SALTY WATER flows away as a deep-water current

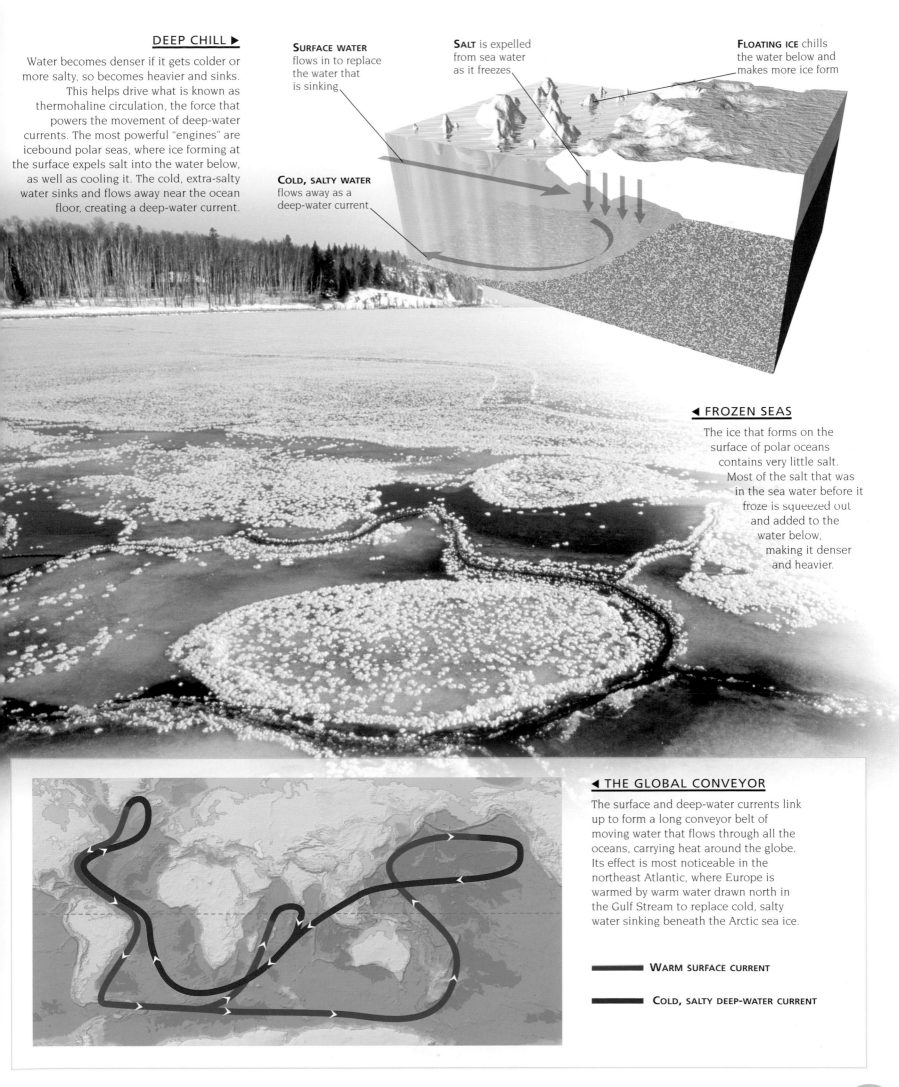

◀ FROZEN SEAS

The ice that forms on the surface of polar oceans contains very little salt. Most of the salt that was in the sea water before it froze is squeezed out and added to the water below, making it denser and heavier.

◀ THE GLOBAL CONVEYOR

The surface and deep-water currents link up to form a long conveyor belt of moving water that flows through all the oceans, carrying heat around the globe. Its effect is most noticeable in the northeast Atlantic, where Europe is warmed by warm water drawn north in the Gulf Stream to replace cold, salty water sinking beneath the Arctic sea ice.

━━━ **WARM SURFACE CURRENT**

━━━ **COLD, SALTY DEEP-WATER CURRENT**

Tides

OCEAN WATER IS HELD ON THE PLANET BY GRAVITY, but it is also attracted by the gravity of the orbiting Moon and drawn toward the Sun. This effect, combined with Earth's 24-hour rotation, causes rising and falling tides. The difference between high and low tide varies with the phases of the Moon, which reflect the Moon's position relative to the Earth and Sun. It also varies with the nature of the sea and coast. Some places like the Bay of Fundy in Canada have huge tidal ranges, while others like the Mediterranean are almost tideless. As the water level rises and falls, it also flows in and out of inlets and along coasts, and in places this can cause navigational hazards such as races and whirlpools.

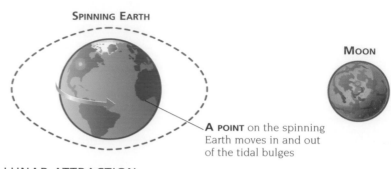

SPINNING EARTH

MOON

A POINT on the spinning Earth moves in and out of the tidal bulges

LUNAR ATTRACTION

The gravitational pull of the Moon drags the ocean toward it, forming a bulge of water that is balanced by another on the opposite side of the world. As the Earth spins, the bulges stay aligned with the Moon, so a particular place such as a beach on the west coast of Africa will move through a bulge zone twice a day. This causes a twice-daily rise and fall of the tide.

UPPER SHORE
Only a few tough animals can survive here

TIDAL ZONES ▶

The rise and fall of the tide creates an intertidal zone, where shore life has to cope with being regularly left high and dry. Only the middle shore near the midtide level is submerged and exposed twice a day. The upper shore is flooded only during high spring tides, and the lower shore is usually underwater. These zones are recognizable by the wildlife that they support.

AT HIGH TIDE, the boats in this harbor, which lies on a coast with a large tidal range, float on deep water.

MIDDLE SHORE
Submerged twice a day, this zone stays wet enough to support a lot of shore life

AT LOW TIDE, six hours later, the boats are almost aground and parts of the harbor have dried out completely.

▲ HIGHS AND LOWS

The tidal rise and fall often varies because of the shape of the coastline. In places where a rising tide is funneled into a narrowing bay, it pushes up farther than on coasts where there is plenty of room for the water to spread out in a thin layer.

LOWER SHORE
Most of the marine life on the shore lives in this zone

◀ SHORE LIFE

The organisms that live on tidal shores are mostly seaweeds and marine animals that have evolved ways of surviving brief exposure to the air. Some can survive for longer than others, and these can live higher up the shore. But since most cannot stay out of the water for long, the much wetter lower shore supports far more species, in greater numbers.

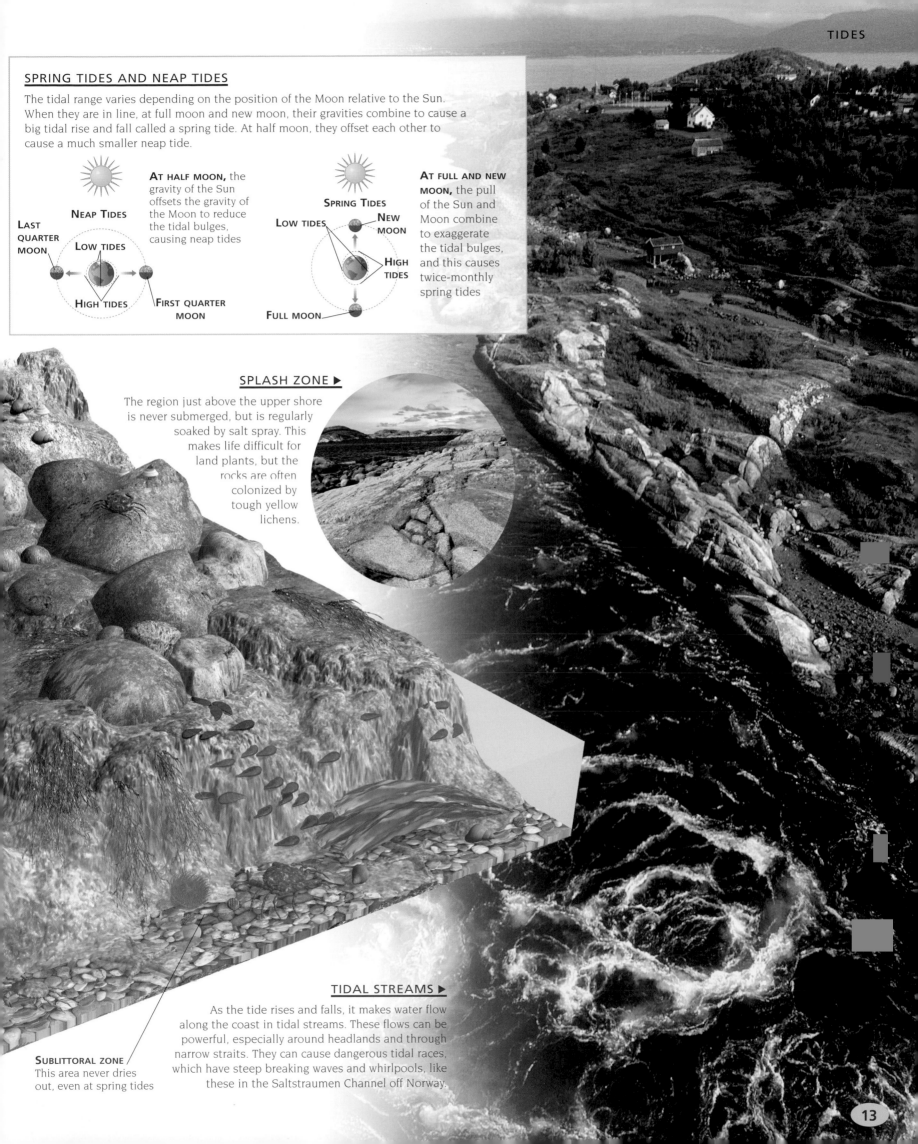

SPRING TIDES AND NEAP TIDES

The tidal range varies depending on the position of the Moon relative to the Sun. When they are in line, at full moon and new moon, their gravities combine to cause a big tidal rise and fall called a spring tide. At half moon, they offset each other to cause a much smaller neap tide.

NEAP TIDES

AT HALF MOON, the gravity of the Sun offsets the gravity of the Moon to reduce the tidal bulges, causing neap tides

LAST QUARTER MOON

LOW TIDES

HIGH TIDES

FIRST QUARTER MOON

SPRING TIDES

LOW TIDES

NEW MOON

HIGH TIDES

FULL MOON

AT FULL AND NEW MOON, the pull of the Sun and Moon combine to exaggerate the tidal bulges, and this causes twice-monthly spring tides

SPLASH ZONE ▶

The region just above the upper shore is never submerged, but is regularly soaked by salt spray. This makes life difficult for land plants, but the rocks are often colonized by tough yellow lichens.

TIDAL STREAMS ▶

As the tide rises and falls, it makes water flow along the coast in tidal streams. These flows can be powerful, especially around headlands and through narrow straits. They can cause dangerous tidal races, which have steep breaking waves and whirlpools, like these in the Saltstraumen Channel off Norway.

SUBLITTORAL ZONE
This area never dries out, even at spring tides

Wind and Wave

WARM AIR over tropical oceans rises and flows toward the poles. Over the subtropics it cools and flows back toward the equator. As the air moves over the surface, the Earth's spin makes it swerve off course, creating the tropical trade winds. Similar effects cause stronger prevailing winds in cooler regions, whipping up big waves. The bands of prevailing winds are divided by calm zones that were dreaded by seamen in the days of sailing ships, because their ships could be stranded there for weeks. The heat of the tropics also generates oceanic storms that can become hurricanes.

▶ PREVAILING WINDS

Dependable prevailing winds blow over wide oceans where there is no land to confuse the pattern. The trade winds in the northern tropics blow from the northeast, while in the south they blow from the southeast. Cooler oceans are swept by westerly winds, while in the polar regions there are cold easterlies .

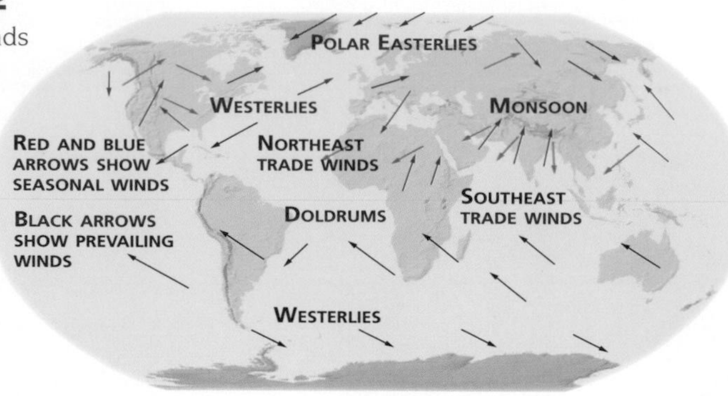

POLAR EASTERLIES
WESTERLIES
MONSOON
RED AND BLUE ARROWS SHOW SEASONAL WINDS
NORTHEAST TRADE WINDS
SOUTHEAST TRADE WINDS
BLACK ARROWS SHOW PREVAILING WINDS
DOLDRUMS
WESTERLIES

CALM ZONES ▶

Prevailing winds are caused by cool air sinking, blowing across the ocean surface as wind, then warming up and rising. The winds are very light in the bands of sinking and rising air, creating calm zones. These move north and south with the seasons, but they are always roughly around the equator—the zone known as the Doldrums—and in the subtropical latitudes at about 30°N and 30°S.

OCEANIC WEATHER ▶

Sun heating the ocean surface makes water turn to water vapor and rise into the air. As it rises it cools and condenses into clouds. This releases energy that warms the air in the cloud, making it rise higher so more water vapor condenses. This process can build up huge storm clouds and creates swirling cyclones that bring wet, windy weather to cooler regions.

EYE OF THE HURRICANE— low air pressure at the center of the hurricane helps create a storm surge that can sweep ashore like a tsunami

▲ HURRICANES

In the tropics the process that forms storm clouds is intensified to create the fierce storms known as hurricanes. Huge clouds and high winds spiral around a calm "eye" at the center, causing torrential rain and ocean storm surges that can swamp coastal cities. This satellite image shows a hurricane moving west across the Gulf of Mexico and battering the Gulf coast of the United States.

◀ OCEAN WAVES

Wind blowing over the ocean drags on its surface to cause waves. These may start as ripples, but they can grow to great heights if the wind is really strong, and the wave can travel for a long distance. The biggest waves build up in broad, windy oceans like the Southern Ocean. However, the *Queen Elizabeth II* encountered a 100-ft (30-m) wave off the coast of Newfoundland in the Atlantic Ocean during Hurricane Luis in 1995.

Cliffs and Beaches

As THEY ARE BATTERED BY OCEAN WAVES, the edges of continents are continually worn away, or eroded. Where rock is undercut at sea level, it collapses to form steep cliffs. The fallen boulders are smashed up into smaller stones and sand, which are swept away and deposited on sheltered shores to form beaches. As more sand and shingle are added to these beaches they may grow in size, extending the coastline out to sea. So while rocky shores are being cut back, beaches are being built up. In the short term, this process creates land as well as destroying it. But over thousands of years the cliffs gradually retreat from the true edges of the continents, creating the continental shelves.

◄ WAVE POWER

When ocean waves roll into shallow water they get shorter and steeper, until their breaking crests finally crash forward onto the shore. The heavy water is forced into cracks in the rock at high pressure, blasting away fragments with explosive force. This gradually wears away the rock at sea level, until the cliffs above collapse into the sea.

▲ BOULDERS AND SAND

The rocks dislodged by the waves are tossed around and their corners are knocked off, creating boulders, shingle, and sand. All these can be moved by water set in motion by the waves, but since it takes more energy to move the heavy boulders, they do not travel far. Lighter shingle and sand are carried farther, into quieter water where they are dropped to form beaches.

HEADLANDS AND BAYS ►

The softer rocks of the coast wear away more easily than hard rocks, creating bays divided by rocky ridges projecting out to sea. These headlands shelter the bays from big waves, encouraging the formation of beaches. So coasts often consist of sandy bays and rocky headlands.

LONGSHORE DRIFT ▶

When waves break on a beach at an angle they dislodge sand and stones and drag them down the beach slope in the backwash. The waves then toss them back on the beach, but farther down the shore. So the beach material is steadily moved along the coast. Over time, this longshore drift can build very long beaches that extend the land out to sea.

THIS LONG SHINGLE BEACH extends for 16 miles (26 km) along the coast of southern England

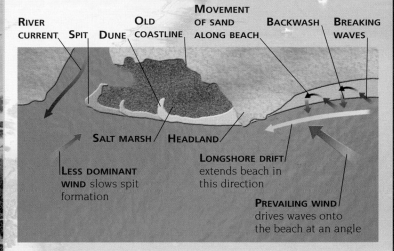

RIVER CURRENT · SPIT · OLD DUNE · COASTLINE · MOVEMENT OF SAND ALONG BEACH · BACKWASH · BREAKING WAVES

SALT MARSH · HEADLAND

LESS DOMINANT WIND slows spit formation

LONGSHORE DRIFT extends beach in this direction

PREVAILING WIND drives waves onto the beach at an angle

EXTENDING THE LAND

As longshore drift carries shingle and sand along the coast, it creates beaches along the shore. In the sheltered waters of a river mouth, where the waves are opposed by the river current, a beach may be built out into open water to form a spit. The area enclosed by the spit is cut off from wave action, and often becomes a muddy salt marsh.

▲ MANGROVES

In the tropics, trees called mangroves are able to grow in the fine sediments that are deposited on sheltered shores as tidal mud. They have tangled roots that slow down water movement and trap more mud, enabling the trees to extend along the coast. These coastal mangroves form important natural barriers against tropical storms.

MUD is deposited when the water stops moving at high tide, and is revealed as the water drains away at low tide

▼ SALT MARSH

The smallest particles of silt and clay stay suspended in the water until they reach sheltered lagoons and river estuaries. Here, where the water is barely moving, they settle to form mudflats. In cool regions the mud near the shore is colonized by salt-tolerant plants to form salt marshes.

Oceanic Gardens

THE BASIC FOOD SOURCE in the open ocean is phytoplankton: clouds of microscopic, drifting plantlike organisms. Like land plants, they use the energy of sunlight to combine carbon dioxide with water to make carbohydrates, in the process of photosynthesis. Phytoplankton make food out of air and water. They are eaten by tiny drifting animals called zooplankton, and both are devoured by shoals of plankton-eating fish and other animals. Predators such as tuna prey on the small fish and are eaten in turn by big hunters like sharks. But the survival of all these animals depends, ultimately, on the phytoplankton.

PHYTOPLANKTON ▶

The clouds of phytoplankton are made up of tiny single-celled organisms, like these diatoms with their glittering shells of glassy silica. They need sunlight to make food, so they are confined to the sunlit zone near the surface. To build their bodies, phytoplankton also need nitrates, phosphates, and other plant nutrients. These tend to settle on the seabed, but are mixed into the water by ocean currents.

PHYTOPLANKTON DENSITY

LEAST DENSE   MOST DENSE

◀ RICH SEAS ▶

If the sunlit surface waters do not contain enough plant nutrients, phytoplankton cannot thrive. The nutrients come from the land or the remains of living things, but in deep oceans they settle on the ocean floor, far below the sunlit zone. In shallow coastal seas the nutrients stored on the seabed reach the surface more easily, and these seas are often a cloudy green because they contain so much microscopic life.

▲ BARREN OCEANS

In tropical oceans the sun warms the surface water and makes it expand, so it weighs less. The lighter, warm water floats on top of the heavier, cold water, and the two do not mix. This stops nutrients from the ocean floor from reaching the sunlit surface. So there is little phytoplankton in most deep tropical oceans, as this satellite image shows, and the water is crystal clear.

▲ UPWELLING ZONES

In some places, powerful wind-driven ocean currents drag deep, cold, nutrient-rich water to the surface. The nutrients fuel the growth of phytoplankton, providing food for masses of zooplankton and fish like these anchovies. These upwelling zones occur off Arabia and along the western coasts of Africa, South America, and North America. Similar equatorial upwelling zones occur in the Atlantic and Pacific.

CORAL OASIS ▶

Tropical ocean water often contains very little phytoplankton, which is why it is so clear. But reef-building corals contain microscopic organisms that also use sunlight to make food. It is these organisms that support the diverse wildlife of coral reefs, which are like submarine oases in clear blue oceanic deserts.

JELLYFISH feeding among the plankton may also be engulfed by the shark

The various types of plankton are eaten by a host of swimming animals, ranging in size from tiny anchovies to penguins and giant blue whales. Many of these animals are filter-feeders like this basking shark. It swims through swarms of plankton with its mouth open, straining tiny animals from the water flowing through its netlike gill rakers.

GILL RAKERS
sieve plankton from the water that flows into the shark's mouth and out through its gills

SWARMS of tiny, mostly transparent animals feast on the microscopic organisms of the phytoplankton

Life in Sunlit Oceans

THE OCEANS PROVIDE a huge 3-D living space for wildlife, but most of this marine life lives in the sunlit zone near the surface. This is because the primary food producers are microscopic phytoplankton, which function rather like plants and need light to survive. The phytoplankton provide food for the tiny animals of the zooplankton, and both types of plankton support larger creatures that may fall prey to hunters. These larger marine animals include fish that swim in open water, crawling animals like crabs and sea stars that live on the bottom, and encrusting and burrowing animals like mussels and worms, which live on the seabed or in the tidal zone on the shore.

ZOOPLANKTON ▶

The microscopic phytoplankton are eaten by drifting swarms of tiny animals called zooplankton. Many of these animals drift in the ocean throughout their lives. They are mainly crustaceans such as copepods and the shrimplike krill of Antarctic waters. Others, like this crab larva, are the young forms of animals that will turn into adults with a different way of life.

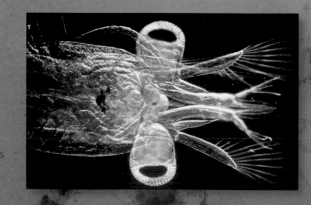

PASSIVE PLANKTON EATERS ▼

Jellyfish, comb jellies, and similar creatures drift with the plankton in open water and eat whatever they run into. Other animals—such as sea anemones, mussels, fanworms, and feather stars—attach themselves to rocks or burrow into soft sand, and filter the water for food.

A COMB JELLY is little more than a tube of jelly with a mouth at one end, but it can engulf animals almost its own size

◀ GRAZERS

Bottom-dwelling animals like limpets, periwinkles, and this spiny sea urchin graze on the seaweeds that grow on submerged rocks. Many meat-eaters such as sea slugs and predatory snails feed in a similar way on encrusting animals that cannot escape from them.

PREDATORS ▶

Many large ocean animals are active hunters that target particular victims. They include fast-swimming open-water fish such as barracuda, tuna, and sharks, as well as less athletic hunters like bottom-dwelling cod, angler fish, and rays. Octopus and squid are also predators, as are seals, dolphins, and many seabirds. The smaller hunters often fall prey to the bigger ones, but top predators like this sand tiger shark have few enemies except man.

LONG, SHARP TEETH of the sand tiger shark are adapted for seizing slippery, struggling fish and preventing their escape

▼ SCAVENGERS

The dead and dying are cleared up by an army of scavengers and debris-eaters that live on the seabed. They include fish, crabs, marine worms, and burrowing clams. In places where there is a lot of food, animals like these brittlestars can live in big, dense colonies.

Life in the Dark

BELOW THE SUNLIT ZONE, there is not enough light to support the living phytoplankton that provide food for animals nearer the surface. The primary food source is edible debris, including dead plankton, that drifts down from above. This is less nutritious than live food, so many small planktonic animals that live in the twilight zone by day migrate toward the surface every night to feed, followed by the fish that eat them. Prey is scarce in the depths, so the dark waters are patrolled by predators with special adaptations for catching anything that wanders across their path. By contrast, most of the creatures of the deep ocean floor are scavengers that eat the remains of dead animals.

EYES of the hatchetfish pick out the silhouettes of prey against the surface

▲ MIGRATING SWARMS

Copepods and other minute planktonic animals make long vertical migrations toward the surface at dusk to feed on phytoplankton, returning to the twilight zone before dawn. They are much safer in the dark, but they are preyed upon by twilight-zone fish, like this hatchetfish, that also migrate toward the surface at night. The migrant swarms attract shoals of plankton-eating fish that feed mainly near the surface, such as herrings and anchovies.

BIG EYES help this deep-sea glass squid see in the gloom of the twilight zone

LIGHT ORGANS behind the transparent squid's eyes can be switched off instantly, so it seems to vanish in the dark

▲ LIGHTS IN THE DARK

Many twilight-zone animals have light organs that glow in the dark. Strangely, these can help conceal them from their enemies. The blue light organs on the belly of a hatchetfish, for example, exactly match the faint blue glow from the surface, disguising the fish's dark silhouette. Other species like these glass squid use light to signal to each other, while hunters use light to lure and even spotlight prey.

TINY COPEPODS less than ¹⁄₁₂ in (2 mm) long make epic upward journeys of up to 1,000 ft (300 m) every night

◀ CHEMICAL ENERGY

Most of the animals living in the dark zone feed on edible debris, or eat each other. But in some places, hot springs welling up from the ocean floor provide bacteria with a source of chemical energy, which they can use to make food. Other animals feed on the bacteria, forming deep-sea communities that live quite independently of the sunlight that supports all other ocean life.

LONG, NEEDLE-SHARP TEETH of this black swallower form a deadly trap, which few animals can escape

▼ ABYSSAL PLAINS

Flat, featureless abyssal plains of soft sediment cover vast areas of ocean floor at depths of 13,000–20,00 ft (4,000–6,000 m). There is no light, the water is close to freezing point, and the pressure is crushing. Despite this, a huge variety of animals, like these sea pens, live on the ocean floor feeding mainly on organic detritus that has drifted down from above.

▲ NIGHTMARE HUNTERS

Food is so scarce in the dark ocean depths that animals such as fish are scarce, too. The predators that live here have to be sure of catching and eating any prey they find, so they have long teeth, huge mouths, and stretchy, balloonlike stomachs that allow them to eat animals that are bigger than they are Yet the bodies of these nightmare hunters are quite small, to reduce the amount of food they need.

Arctic Ocean

UNLIKE THE ANTARCTIC, which is a frozen continent surrounded by ocean, the Arctic is centered on a frozen ocean surrounded by continents. The North Pole itself is a point on the ocean floor, and it lies beneath floating ice that is moving all the time, driven by currents that flow clockwise around the ocean. The ocean floor has several deep basins fringed by broad shallow seas on the Asian side, and an archipelago of islands on the Canadian side. It is divided by the Arctic Midocean Ridge, which is an extension of the Mid-Atlantic Ridge. This is a site of active ocean-floor spreading, which is pushing Asia away from North America and Greenland, so the Arctic Ocean is getting larger every year.

26–27 POLAR ICE SHEET

The central Arctic Ocean is covered by a sheet of floating ice, built up from ice floes driven together by winds and currents. The ice forms near Siberia and drifts slowly across the North Pole before melting, so the ice is being continuously replaced. Around the fringes of this year-round ice the ocean surface freezes in winter and melts in summer, so the ice sheet gets bigger and smaller. Marine animals feed at the edge of the ice, moving south and north as the ice sheet expands and contracts.

The most powerful Arctic predator, the polar bear spends most of its time on the floating sea ice hunting for seals.

28–29 SIBERIAN SEAS

A broad continental shelf extends along the northern edge of Asia, and into the Bering Sea. The shallow, fertile shelf seas bloom with microscopic life in summer, providing food for fish and bottom-dwelling animals such as clams, and these are eaten by seals and whales. In winter, the Siberian seas freeze over, creating a continuous sheet of ice extending to the North Pole. Much of the wildlife retreats to the ice-free waters of the Bering Sea and Barents Sea, returning in spring when the winter ice starts to melt and break up.

Huge, powerful icebreakers plow a channel through the sea ice near the shores of Siberia to link the northern ports.

30–31 CANADIAN ARCTIC ISLANDS

The continental shelf linking Canada to northern Greenland is dotted with islands. They are separated by channels that freeze over in winter, except for patches of open water known as polynas. The northern islands are icy deserts, but the southern islands support huge breeding colonies of seabirds in summer, as well as animals such as caribou and wolves.

Floating icebergs drift through the Arctic seas around Greenland, making navigation difficult and dangerous.

North Pacific Basin

PACIFIC OCEAN

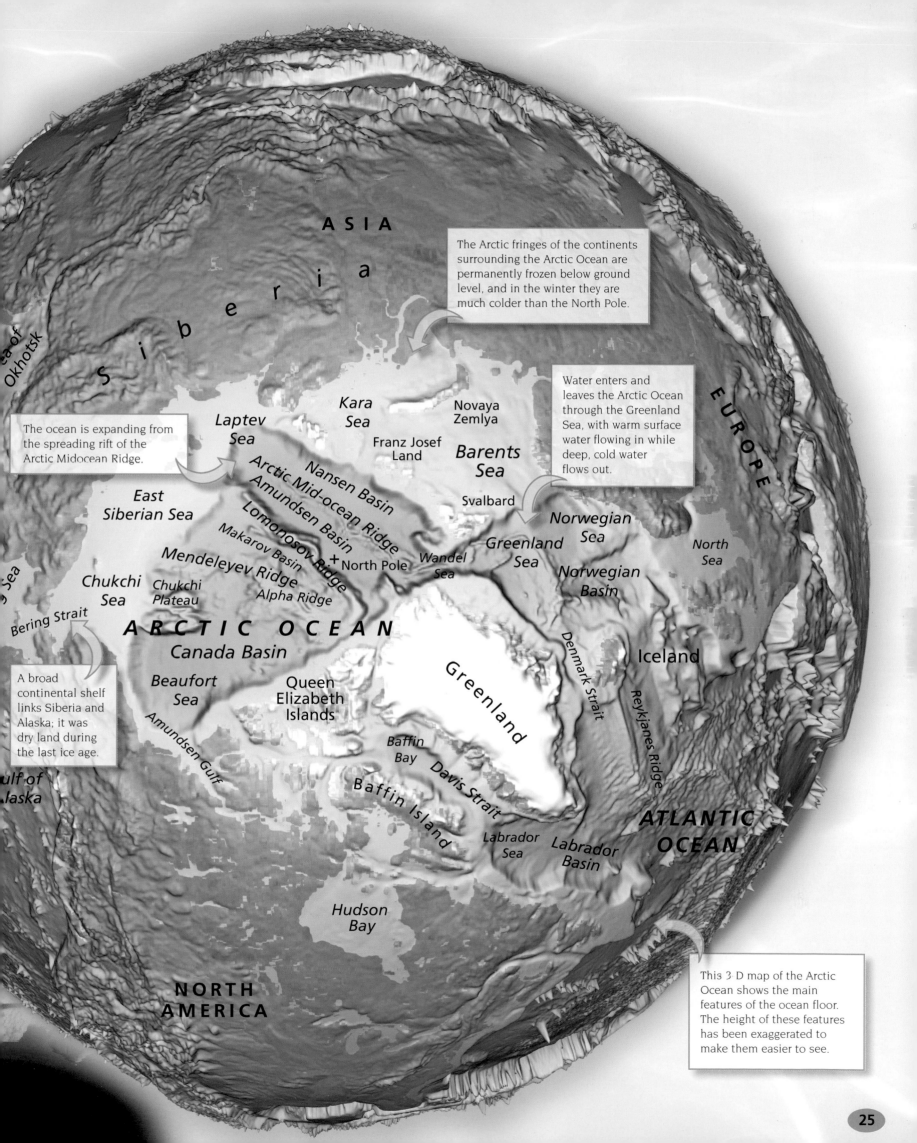

ASIA

The Arctic fringes of the continents surrounding the Arctic Ocean are permanently frozen below ground level, and in the winter they are much colder than the North Pole.

Sea of Okhotsk

S i b e r i a

Water enters and leaves the Arctic Ocean through the Greenland Sea, with warm surface water flowing in while deep, cold water flows out.

Kara Sea

Novaya Zemlya

EUROPE

The ocean is expanding from the spreading rift of the Arctic Midocean Ridge.

Laptev Sea

Franz Josef Land

Barents Sea

Nansen Basin

Arctic Mid-ocean Ridge

East Siberian Sea

Amundsen Basin

Lomonosov Ridge

Makarov Basin

Svalbard

Norwegian Sea

North Sea

Mendeleyev Ridge

+ North Pole

Greenland Sea

Wandel Sea

Norwegian Basin

Chukchi Sea

Chukchi Plateau

Alpha Ridge

Bering Strait

Denmark Strait

Iceland

ARCTIC OCEAN

Reykjanes Ridge

Canada Basin

A broad continental shelf links Siberia and Alaska; it was dry land during the last ice age.

Beaufort Sea

Queen Elizabeth Islands

Greenland

Gulf of Alaska

Amundsen Gulf

Baffin Bay

Davis Strait

ATLANTIC OCEAN

Baffin Island

Labrador Sea

Labrador Basin

Hudson Bay

NORTH AMERICA

This 3-D map of the Arctic Ocean shows the main features of the ocean floor. The height of these features has been exaggerated to make them easier to see.

Polar Ice Sheet

THE ICE THAT FLOATS ON THE ARCTIC OCEAN forms as a continuous sheet in winter, but soon cracks up into separate ice floes. These are driven together by winds and currents, which pile them up into thick pack ice that drifts slowly across the North Pole. The ice melts as it moves away from the polar region, and the thinner ice around the fringes melts in summer. Only the central area is covered by ice all year, although as climate change makes the Arctic Ocean warmer, even this summer ice may melt in the future. Whales, seals, and polar bears feed near the edge of the floating ice, so migrate toward the North Pole as the ice sheet shrinks in summer, and away from it as the ice expands in winter.

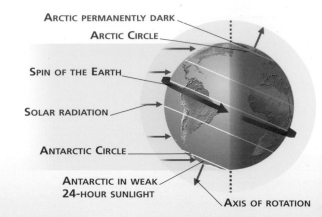

ARCTIC PERMANENTLY DARK
ARCTIC CIRCLE
SPIN OF THE EARTH
SOLAR RADIATION
ANTARCTIC CIRCLE
ANTARCTIC IN WEAK 24-HOUR SUNLIGHT
AXIS OF ROTATION

ARCTIC WINTERS

At midwinter the North Pole is tilted away from the Sun, so the whole of the Arctic is in 24-hour darkness. This allows temperatures to drop well below freezing, to the point where the sea's surface turns to ice. At midsummer there is 24-hour sunlight, but the Sun is so low in the sky that it does not have enough power to melt all the ice.

▲ MOVING TARGET

Sea ice is constantly moving across the North Pole, as currents drive it clockwise around the ocean. This means that the sign that marks the North Pole is always drifting away from its correct position, and it has to be regularly pulled out of the ice and moved.

◀ RINGED SEAL

The most northerly of the Arctic seals, the ringed seal hunts beneath the ice for fish such as Arctic cod, coming up for air at breathing holes. It breeds in spring, inside ice caves in the piled-up pack ice, but many pups are caught and eaten by polar bears.

Fridtjof Nansen

In the 1890s, this Norwegian scientist allowed his ship to become frozen into the Arctic pack ice. The ship drifted over the North Pole, proving that polar ice drifted too.

DENSE WHITE FUR and a thick layer of fat protect the bear from the cold air and water.

▶ ICE BEAR

The polar bear hunts seals on the frozen ocean, following the edge of the thick pack ice as it expands and contracts with the seasons. It has trouble finding enough food on land, and if the summer sea ice ever melts altogether because of global warming, the polar bear could become extinct.

▲ TUSKED WHALE

The narwhal lives in deep Arctic waters, along the edge of the pack ice that advances and retreats throughout the year. It is famous for the single long, spiral tusk of the male, which grows to a length of 6 ft (2 m) or more. Rival males sometimes spar with their tusks, as seen here.

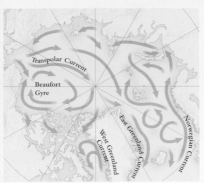

COLD AIR sinks over the Arctic ice and flows away from the North Pole as surface wind. But the spin of the Earth makes the wind swerve to the west, so it blows from the east. These cold easterlies drive the surface waters of the Arctic Ocean, and the floating ice, clockwise around the pole. Water also enters and leaves the Arctic Ocean through the gap between Greenland and Scandinavia.

EVERY SUMMER huge areas of Arctic sea ice melt away. But as ocean temperatures have risen, more ice has melted each year. Since the 1980s, the size of the ice sheet in September has dwindled by about 500,000 sq miles (1.3 million sq km). If this dramatic trend continues, summers at the North Pole could be completely ice-free by 2070.

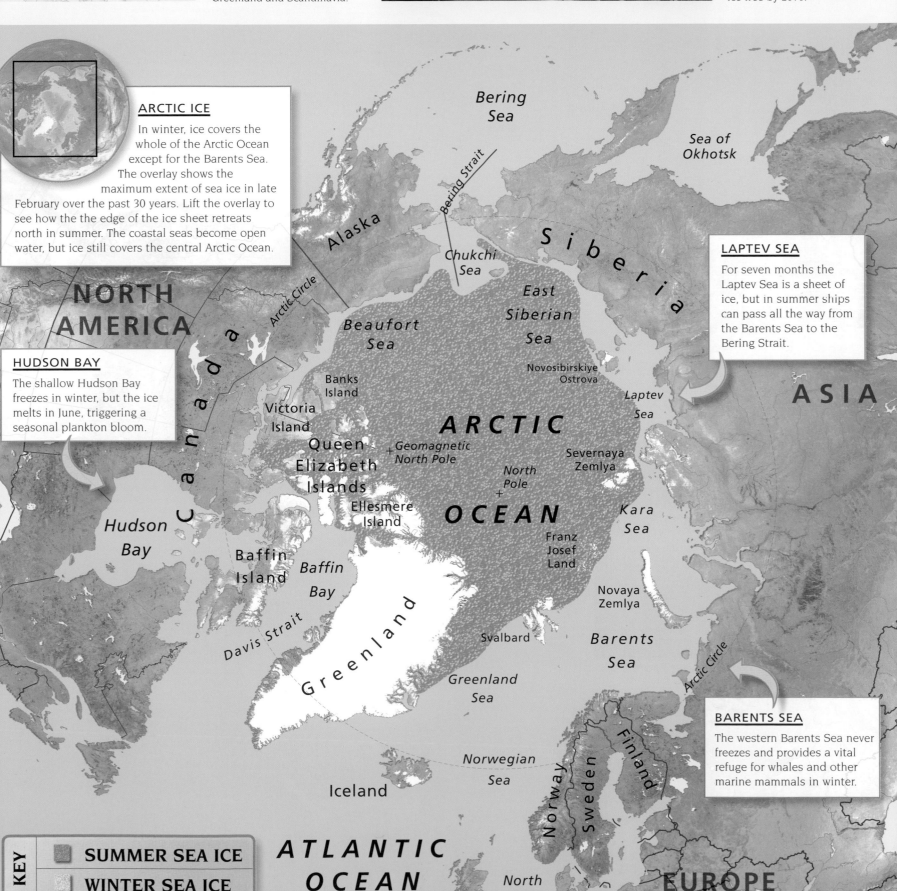

ARCTIC ICE

In winter, ice covers the whole of the Arctic Ocean except for the Barents Sea. The overlay shows the maximum extent of sea ice in late February over the past 30 years. Lift the overlay to see how the the edge of the ice sheet retreats north in summer. The coastal seas become open water, but ice still covers the central Arctic Ocean.

HUDSON BAY

The shallow Hudson Bay freezes in winter, but the ice melts in June, triggering a seasonal plankton bloom.

LAPTEV SEA

For seven months the Laptev Sea is a sheet of ice, but in summer ships can pass all the way from the Barents Sea to the Bering Strait.

BARENTS SEA

The western Barents Sea never freezes and provides a vital refuge for whales and other marine mammals in winter.

NORTH AMERICA

Canada

Alaska

Arctic Circle

Bering Sea

Sea of Okhotsk

Bering Strait

Chukchi Sea

S i b e r i a

East Siberian Sea

Beaufort Sea

Banks Island

Victoria Island

Queen Elizabeth Islands

Ellesmere Island

+ *Geomagnetic North Pole*

North Pole +

ARCTIC OCEAN

Novosibirskiye Ostrova

Laptev Sea

Severnaya Zemlya

Kara Sea

Franz Josef Land

Novaya Zemlya

ASIA

Hudson Bay

Baffin Island

Baffin Bay

Davis Strait

Greenland

Greenland Sea

Svalbard

Barents Sea

Arctic Circle

Norway

Sweden

Finland

Iceland

Norwegian Sea

ATLANTIC OCEAN

North Sea

EUROPE

KEY

SUMMER SEA ICE

WINTER SEA ICE

Siberian Seas

THE DEEP BASINS OF THE CENTRAL ARCTIC OCEAN are flanked on the Asian side by a broad continental shelf, extending up to 600 miles (1,000 km) from the Siberian coast. The shallow seas over the continental shelf freeze in winter, but melt near the coast in summer to allow wildlife access to the food-rich waters below. Huge rivers flow off Asia into these Siberian seas, and in spring the meltwater draining off Siberia turns the inshore waters of the Laptev Sea almost fresh. Global warming is increasing the freshwater flow, and this could eventually disrupt ocean currents in the far north.

◀ WHITE WHALE

The gleaming white beluga is an Arctic whale that hunts fish, squid, and crabs in shallow coastal waters, swimming in company and communicating with chirps and whistles. When the sea freezes in the fall, belugas move south to ice-free regions like the Bering Sea. In the spring they follow the melting edge of the pack ice as it retreats north, back into the Arctic Ocean.

WALRUS TUSKS are social symbols, like the antlers of deer—the longer they are, the higher the animal's status

WALRUS HERDS ▶

These heavyweight, thick-skinned seals feed in shallow Arctic seas, using their whiskery snouts to root around on the seabed for clams and other shellfish. They often haul out of the sea to rest in big herds on island beaches, especially in late summer, when there is not much sea ice for them to lie on.

▲ SPRING BLOOM

The Siberian seas are so shallow that nutrients are easily stirred up from the seabed and mixed with the water, making it very fertile. The phytoplankton lie dormant all winter and start multiplying rapidly when the pack ice breaks up in spring. This spring bloom causes a population explosion among zooplankton, providing a feast for fish throughout the summer.

SUNLIGHT penetrates the thin, broken ice in spring, illuminating the water and triggering a plankton bloom

DID YOU KNOW?

The frozen Laptev Sea has been called the ice factory of the Arctic, because it generates most of the floating pack ice that forms the ice sheet at the North Pole.

▼ FLOWERING TUNDRA

In summer the snow on the coastal tundra melts, exposing the tough, low-growing Arctic vegetation. The plants burst into flower, and swarms of insects hatch. The insects are eaten by flocks of shorebirds, geese, and wild swans that migrate north in spring to nest on the tundra, and the birds—and their eggs and chicks—provide prey for prowling Arctic foxes.

TUNDRA PLANTS spend the winter buried by snow, their roots in frozen ground

THE DARK FUR that the Arctic fox sports in summer turns pure white in winter

▼ ICEBREAKER FLEET

The ports on the Arctic shores of Russia and Siberia are linked by the 3,000-mile (5,000-km) Northern Sea Route. This is kept free of ice for as long as possible by a fleet of more than 75 icebreakers. The specially strengthened ships ride up on the sea ice as they are driven forward, and break the ice with their immense weight.

▲ ALASKAN OIL

Alaska forms the eastern shore of the shallow Chukchi Sea, but its northern coast lies on the edge of the deep Canada Basin. This is the site of the Prudhoe Bay oilfield that was discovered in 1968, the largest in North America. The oil is pumped across Alaska to the port of Valdez on the north Pacific, through a 800-mile (1,290-km) pipeline.

Canadian Arctic Islands

THE NORTHERN ISLANDS are divided from the rest of Arctic Canada by the deep Parry Channel. This marks a geological frontier between the ancient rocks of the south, known as the Canadian Shield, and the more recent rocks of the Arctic islands.

TO THE EAST OF ALASKA, the Arctic Ocean is fringed by the islands of the Canadian Arctic archipelago, which lie on the continental shelf linking Canada and northern Greenland. The channels between the islands are icebound in winter, so they form an extension of the Arctic ice sheet, but in summer much of the sea ice breaks up and melts. This allows sunlight to flood into the water, which is rich in nutrients and oxygen, creating a summer bloom of plankton. The resulting mass of food is exploited by fish, which attract whales, seals, and huge numbers of seabirds.

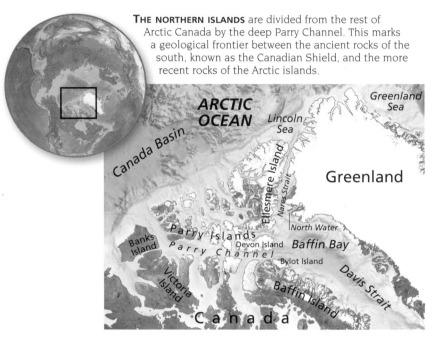

ARCTIC OCEAN
Greenland Sea
Lincoln Sea
Canada Basin
Greenland
Greenland
Ellesmere Island
Nares Strait
North Water
Parry Islands
Banks Island
Devon Island
Baffin Bay
Parry Channel
Bylot Island
Victoria Island
Baffin Island
Davis Strait
Canada

◄ ICEBOUND ISLANDS

In winter the islands are covered with snow and surrounded by sea ice, so they seem to form part of a continuous ice sheet, punctuated by dark patches of open water. In spring the snow and ice start to retreat, the stretches of open water get bigger, and the land starts to turn green, as in this satellite image of Devon Island in June.

ISLAND LIFE ▼

There is continuous permafrost on the Arctic islands, but a shallow surface layer thaws in summer and refreezes in the following winter. This gives grass and tough cushion plants like purple saxifrage a chance to grow, providing food for musk oxen, caribou, and Arctic hares. These grazers are hunted in turn by Arctic wolves.

ARCTIC HARE is one of the few animals that can survive a winter on the polar fringes of the Arctic

▲ COASTAL BIRDS

Millions of gulls, fulmars, terns, and other seabirds like these Brünnich's guillemots form breeding colonies on the craggy island coasts in spring. They feed their young on plankton and fish gathered from the channels where the sea ice has melted.

◀ POLYNA

As the sea ice retreats in spring, many patches of open water, known as polynas, appear. Some of these, such as North Water in the north of Baffin Bay, also stay open throughout the winter. Their waters are very productive, providing rich feeding habitats for marine wildlife such as bowhead whales, ringed seals, and polar bears, as well as seabirds that have migrated north to breed.

LEAD ▶

Broad channels, or leads, open up in the sea ice in late spring. These provide migration routes for marine mammals like these beluga whales, enabling them to swim to new feeding grounds that have been cut off by ice throughout the winter. They cannot migrate long distances under the ice, because they must surface regularly to breathe.

ARCTIC PEOPLES ▲

This region is the home of the Inuit, who until recently were self-sufficient hunters who used simple weapons. Today they hunt with rifles, traveling by motorized sled and boat. This is dramatically affecting Arctic wildlife to the extent that certain seabird colonies have already been wiped out.

DRIFTING ICEBERGS ▼

Many glaciers on the Arctic islands and Greenland reach the coast, where great chunks of ice break off to float away as icebergs. Ocean currents carry many of these south from Baffin Bay to the Davis Strait, and into the north Atlantic.

DID YOU KNOW?

Northern Ellesmere Island in the Canadian Arctic is a polar desert, drier than parts of the Sahara. This is because the permanent ice covering the Arctic Ocean stops water from evaporating and forming snow clouds.

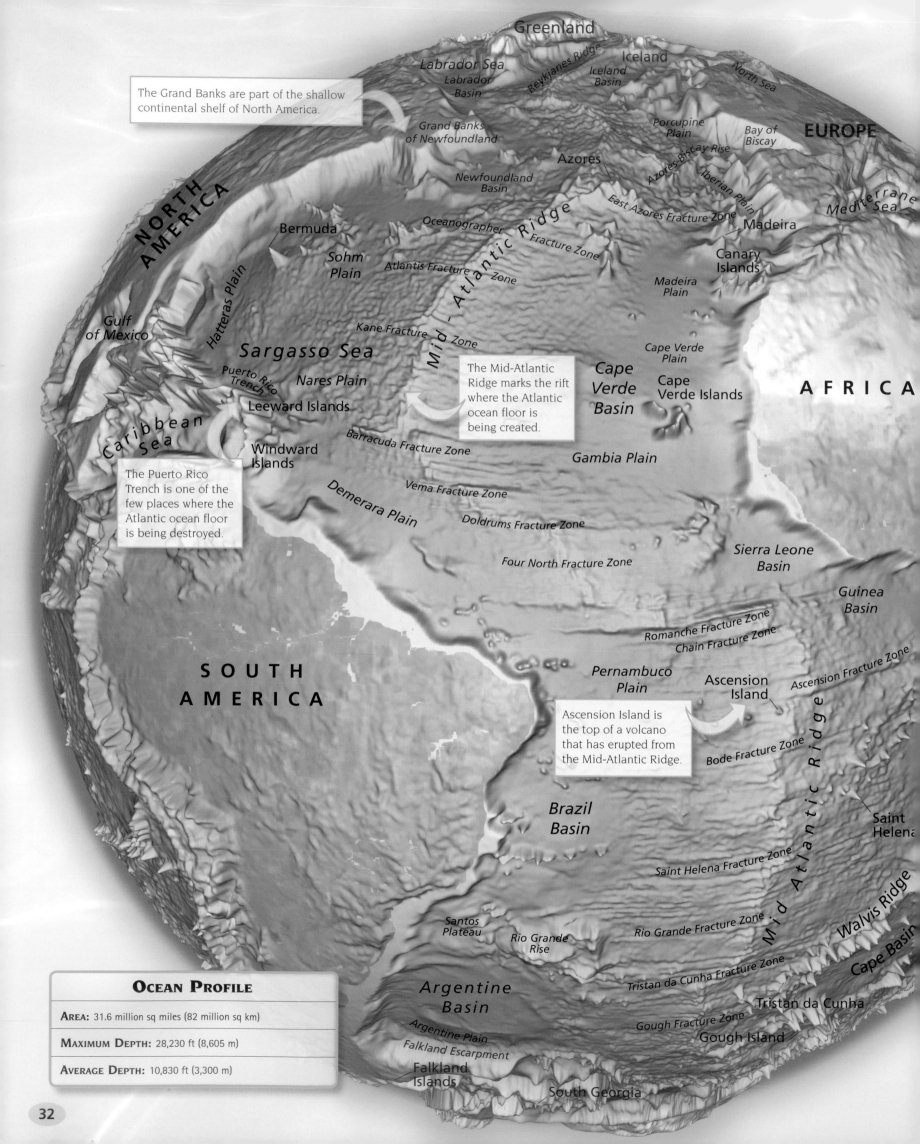

Greenland

Labrador Sea
Labrador
Basin

Iceland

Reykjanes Ridge

Iceland
Basin

North
Sea

EUROPE

The Grand Banks are part of the shallow continental shelf of North America.

Grand Banks
of Newfoundland

Porcupine
Plain

Bay of
Biscay

NORTH
AMERICA

Newfoundland
Basin

Azores

Azores-Biscay Rise

East Azores Fracture Zone

Iberian Plain

Mediterranean
Sea

Bermuda

Oceanographer
Fracture Zone

Madeira

Sohm
Plain

Atlantis Fracture Zone

Canary
Islands

Madeira
Plain

Gulf
of Mexico

Hatteras Plain

Kane Fracture Zone

Mid-Atlantic Ridge

Cape Verde
Plain

Sargasso Sea

Cape
Verde
Basin

The Mid-Atlantic Ridge marks the rift where the Atlantic ocean floor is being created.

Cape
Verde Islands

AFRICA

Puerto Rico
Trench

Nares Plain

Leeward Islands

Caribbean
Sea

Windward
Islands

Barracuda Fracture Zone

Gambia Plain

The Puerto Rico Trench is one of the few places where the Atlantic ocean floor is being destroyed.

Demerara Plain

Vema Fracture Zone

Doldrums Fracture Zone

Sierra Leone
Basin

Four North Fracture Zone

Guinea
Basin

SOUTH
AMERICA

Romanche Fracture Zone

Chain Fracture Zone

Pernambuco
Plain

Ascension
Island

Ascension Fracture Zone

Ascension Island is the top of a volcano that has erupted from the Mid-Atlantic Ridge.

Bode Fracture Zone

Mid-Atlantic Ridge

Brazil
Basin

Saint
Helena

Saint Helena Fracture Zone

Santos
Plateau

Rio Grande
Rise

Rio Grande Fracture Zone

Mid-Atlantic Ridge

Walvis Ridge

Argentine
Basin

Tristan da Cunha Fracture Zone

Cape Basin

Argentine Plain

Falkland Escarpment

Gough Fracture Zone

Tristan da Cunha

Gough Island

Falkland
Islands

South Georgia

OCEAN PROFILE

AREA: 31.6 million sq miles (82 million sq km)

MAXIMUM DEPTH: 28,230 ft (8,605 m)

AVERAGE DEPTH: 10,830 ft (3,300 m)

Atlantic Ocean

THE ATLANTIC HAS DEVELOPED from a spreading rift between Europe and Africa on one side, and North and South America on the other. The rift is marked by the Mid-Atlantic Ridge, which extends from near Antarctica to beyond Iceland. All the ocean floor of the Atlantic has been created in the last 175 million years, which means that the ocean did not exist until halfway through the Jurassic Period in the age of dinosaurs. The ocean floor is still expanding at just over 1⅕ in (3 cm) a year, and has created the Puerto Rico Trench, where it dives beneath the Caribbean Plate. Meanwhile, the Mediterranean is getting smaller as Africa pushes up toward Europe.

ack Sea

São Tomé

This 3-D map of the Atlantic Ocean shows the main features of the ocean floor. The height of these features has been exaggerated to make them easier to see.

40–41 MEDITERRANEAN AND BLACK SEA

Ancient wrecks litter the seabed near rocky Mediterranean shores.

The coasts of these virtually landlocked seas are dotted with beautiful cities and the ruins of past civilizations.

42–43 TROPICAL NORTH ATLANTIC

The clear blue tropical oceans contain little life compared with the gray-green northern and coastal seas. In the Sargasso Sea in central north Atlantic, most of the marine life is concentrated at the surface.

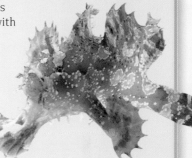

The sargassum fish lives invisibly among floating seaweed.

44–45 CARIBBEAN

Notorious for its hurricanes, the Caribbean is also a region of beautiful coral-fringed tropical islands.

A satellite view of an approaching hurricane.

46–47 GULF OF MEXICO

Huge oil reserves make the Gulf of Mexico vital to the United States economy, but Gulf coasts are threatened by rising sea levels and storms.

Hundreds of offshore oil rigs dot the waters of the Gulf.

48–49 WEST AFRICAN SEAS

Cold, nutrient-rich waters off the Atlantic coast of southern Africa support huge shoals of fish that attract some of the world's biggest marine animals.

A diving sperm whale slips from sight.

34–35 NORTHWEST ATLANTIC

The rich shelf seas off Newfoundland are among the most famous fisheries in the world, but icebergs drifting south from the Arctic make these waters hazardous for shipping.

Cod fishing on the Grand Banks is strictly controlled to conserve fish stocks.

36–37 MID–ATLANTIC RIDGE

Surtsey erupted from the Mid-Atlantic Ridge just south of Iceland in 1963.

The volcanic midocean ridge is most active in the north Atlantic, rising above sea level to form Iceland.

38–39 NORTHEAST ATLANTIC

The shallow coastal waters of the northeast Atlantic have been important trading routes for centuries, helping to create the wealth of the European nations. They teem with marine life despite decades of overfishing, and there are huge oil and gas reserves beneath the bed of the North Sea.

The food-rich waters support huge breeding colonies of seabirds like this Atlantic puffin, seen here with fish that it has caught.

Northwest Atlantic

THE WATERS OF NEWFOUNDLAND in eastern Canada are rich in marine life, thanks to the interaction of warm and cold ocean currents over the broad, shallow continental shelf of the Grand Banks. But the cold Labrador Current also creates conditions that lead to the winter freezing of the Gulf of St. Lawrence to the west of Newfoundland, and carries icebergs south from Greenland into the busy shipping routes of the Atlantic.

THE ICY LABRADOR CURRENT flows south from the Arctic to cross the Grand Banks, a broad area of continental shelf that lies between the deep Labrador Basin and the North American Basin.

◀ FISHING WATERS

The Grand Banks extend 250 miles (400 km) off the coast of Newfoundland, and lie just 80–330 ft (25–100 m) below the surface. The mixing of the cold Labrador Current with the warm Gulf Stream helps draw nutrients up from the shallow seabed, resulting in clouds of plankton that support masses of marine life. These waters were once the most famous fisheries in the world, but they have suffered badly from overfishing.

◀ VIKING SETTLEMENT

In 985, more than 500 years before Columbus, a Viking ship reached Newfoundland after being driven southwest from Greenland by a storm. The Vikings later settled on the northern tip of the island, where their turf-roofed houses have now been recreated.

▼ ICY NURSERY

Frozen in winter, the Gulf of St. Lawrence to the west of Newfoundland is a breeding site for hundreds of thousands of harp seals. The female seals climb out onto the ice in late February to give birth to their pups, and feed them on their very rich milk.

WHITE-FURRED PUPS are fed on milk for just 12 days before being left to fend for themselves

▲ ICEBERG!

The mighty ship *Titanic* was on her first transatlantic voyage in April 1912 when she collided with an iceberg carried south by the Labrador Current. The ship took nearly three hours to sink, but because she did not carry enough lifeboats, some 1,500 people died in the freezing water. In 1985 the wreck was discovered lying 12,470 ft (3,800 m) below the surface, off the southern tip of the Grand Banks.

◀ RECORD TIDES

The Bay of Fundy in eastern Canada has the highest tides in the world, caused by tidal water surging up the channel from the Gulf of Maine. In six hours the water can rise over 50 ft (16 m), and the rocks at Hopewell Cape have been carved into fantastic shapes by the tidal streams.

BOWHEADED WHALES were among the main species hunted

▲ NANTUCKET WHALERS

The rich, shallow seas of the Grand Banks attract whales that feed on the abundant fish. In the past these whales were hunted from nearby ports such as Nantucket, near Boston. These early whalers used simple hand harpoons hurled from open rowing boats, which was extremely dangerous. Many whaling boats were capsized and lost in the cold, gray waters.

DID YOU KNOW?

▶ This area of the north Atlantic often suffers massive storms in the fall, as cold air from Canada interacts with warm air over the Atlantic. One of these storms sank the boat *Andrea Gail* in October 1991, inspiring the book and film *The Perfect Storm*.

Mid-Atlantic Ridge

THE FLOOR OF THE ATLANTIC OCEAN is divided by the submarine mountain chain of the Mid-Atlantic Ridge, created by a volcanic, spreading rift that is pushing America away from Europe and Africa. A hotspot beneath part of the northern ridge has raised it above the waves to form Iceland, with its many active volcanoes and scalding hot geysers. One side of Iceland lies on the North American plate, while the other side is part of Europe.

THE VOLCANIC ISLAND OF ICELAND is an exposed part of the Reykjanes Ridge, which is a northern extension of the Mid-Atlantic Ridge. The ridge system continues north from Iceland across the Arctic Ocean.

▼ DIVIDED LAND

The rift valley that runs down the center of the Mid-Atlantic Ridge passes straight through Iceland. At Thingvellir in the southwest it forms a broad, flat valley flanked by steep cliffs. The floor of the valley is covered with basalt lava erupted from the spreading rift.

CLIFFS on the western side of the rift mark the edge of the North American plate

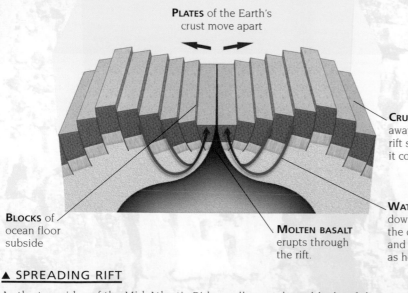

PLATES of the Earth's crust move apart

CRUST moving away from the rift sinks as it cools

BLOCKS of ocean floor subside

MOLTEN BASALT erupts through the rift.

WATER seeps down through the cracks and erupts as hot springs

▲ SPREADING RIFT

As the two sides of the Mid-Atlantic Ridge pull apart, huge blocks of the ocean floor subside into the mantle below, creating a central rift valley. But the heat of the magma chamber beneath the rift makes the rocks expand, raising the cracked blocks on each side into a double ridge.

◄ OCEANIC VOLCANOES

Iceland is the most active part of the Mid-Atlantic Ridge system, with dozens of active volcanoes that have spilled a vast amount of dark basalt lava onto the island. One of the largest, Grímsvötn, is largely covered by a thick ice cap, and heat from the volcano frequently causes destructive floods of meltwater. Surtsey, seen here, erupted from the Reykjanes Ridge off the southwest coast of Iceland, appearing above the waves in 1963.

MIGRATING WHOOPER SWANS may fly 750 miles (1,200 km) nonstop from Great Britain to Iceland.

▲ GEOTHERMAL ENERGY

Water draining down into the hot core of Iceland is superheated under pressure until it bursts up in hot geysers. The same heat source has been tapped to provide hot water for towns such as the Icelandic capital, Reykjavik, and to run geothermal power plants that generate electricity.

▲ SUMMER VISITORS

Despite its cold climate and volcanic dangers, Iceland is rich in wildlife. Large numbers of shorebirds and wildfowl migrate to the island each summer to breed and take advantage of the virtually continuous summer daylight to find the food that they need.

VALLEY FLOOR of the rift is sinking at the rate of 4 in (10 cm) a century

DID YOU KNOW?

▶ In 1783, a crack in the Icelandic rift system called the Laki fissure erupted about 3.5 cubic miles (15 cubic km) of lava and poison gas. More than 9,000 people died as a result.

Northeast Atlantic

NORTHERN EUROPE IS SURROUNDED by shallow shelf seas, which are warmed by the Gulf Stream flowing northeast from Florida. This helps to maintain a mild, moist climate that is ideal for growing crops, forming the basis of the wealth that made Europe a center of civilization for some 3,000 years. The long coastlines are dotted with fishing and trading ports, which from the days of the Vikings were used as bases for ocean exploration.

DURING THE LAST ICE AGE the British Isles were attached to Europe. But when the ice melted the sea level rose, flooding the continental shelf to create the shallow English Channel and North Sea.

◄ MARITIME CLIMATE

Although Great Britain lies to the north of the Gulf of St. Lawrence in Canada, which freezes in winter, the climate of the Scilly Isles in the southwest is warm enough to grow tropical palm trees. This is partly because the prevailing westerly winds carry mild oceanic weather over the land, preventing the frosts that would kill the trees—but also because the air temperature is raised by the warm Gulf Stream current.

WINTER FLOCKS ►

The mild oceanic winters attract millions of shorebirds like these dunlins, which breed in the far north in summer, then migrate south and west to form huge winter flocks on sandy bays and estuaries.

RICH SHELF SEAS ▶

Nutrients scoured from the shallow sea floor by seasonal storms fuel plankton growth, which once provided food for vast numbers of fish. But overfishing and rising sea temperatures caused by climate change have virtually destroyed many fish populations. Some breeding colonies of seabirds like this puffin are in serious trouble, because the birds cannot catch enough small fish to feed their young.

SANDEELS are vital food for puffins, but are becoming difficult to find

NORTH SEA OIL ▶

In the North Sea, the remains of ancient marine organisms sealed beneath the rocks of the sea floor have generated huge reserves of oil and natural gas. Despite the difficulties and dangers, the reserves are tapped by more than 400 offshore drilling platforms.

BRACKISH BALTIC ▶

The waters of the almost landlocked Baltic are not as salty as the North Sea. Many marine animals cannot survive, including the shipworm that destroys wrecked wooden ships. This explains the preservation of the Swedish galleon *Vasa*, which sank in Stockholm harbor in 1628 and was raised virtually intact 333 years later.

▲ RECLAIMED LAND

Much of the land seen in this satellite image of the Netherlands lies below sea level and has been reclaimed from the sea. Surrounded by dykes and pumped dry, it now makes fertile farmland. The large area of water in the center of the image is also cut off from the sea by a dyke, and may be drained one day.

COASTAL TERRACE at Rhossili in South Wales, now used as farmland, was once a beach lapped by the waves

RISING CONTINENTS ▶

The thick sheets of ice that covered the northern lands during the last ice age weighed down the Earth's crust, and since they melted away the land has been slowly springing up again. This has lifted ancient shorelines well above sea level, creating features like this raised beach.

Mediterranean and Black Sea

ONE OF THE WORLD'S BUSIEST SEAS, the Mediterranean has been a center of civilization and international trade for thousands of years. It is still a major route for shipping, much of it carrying oil through the Suez Canal from the Middle East. The people who live around its shores are augmented by huge numbers of tourists who visit the region each summer to enjoy its sunny climate and rich culture. The tourist trade brings wealth, but it also causes problems by encouraging the construction of badly planned coastal resorts. This increases the marine pollution that is becoming a serious threat to fish and other wildlife, as well as to the tourists themselves.

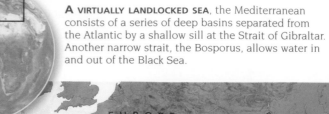

A VIRTUALLY LANDLOCKED SEA, the Mediterranean consists of a series of deep basins separated from the Atlantic by a shallow sill at the Strait of Gibraltar. Another narrow strait, the Bosporus, allows water in and out of the Black Sea.

A FIRE FOUNTAIN of hot rock and molten lava explodes from Mount Etna during an eruption

◄ VOLCANO BELT

The Mediterranean is the remains of an ancient ocean called the Tethys, which has been reduced to a relatively small sea as Africa has drifted north to collide with Europe. The collision has pushed up the sea floor to form the Mediterranean Ridge and causes regular earthquakes along a seismic belt studded with volcanoes such as Vesuvius, Etna, and Santorini.

ISLAND RESORTS ►

The glorious landscapes, ancient cities, relaxed lifestyle, and fine food of the Mediterranean region have been celebrated in literature for nearly 3,000 years. They draw many tourists to its coasts and islands, and tourism has become vital to the economy of places like Mallorca in the Balearic Islands.

ROCKY ISLANDS in the Mediterranean generally have thin, infertile soils, so much of their natural wealth comes from the sea

Jacques Cousteau

The scuba diving gear that has enabled so many people to explore the ocean for themselves was coinvented in 1943 by French diver Jacques Cousteau (1910–1997), who did much of his pioneering work in the Mediterranean. He later became famous for his many TV films about the undersea world.

◄ THREATENED WILDLIFE

The wildlife of the Mediterranean includes spectacular animals like swordfish, giant tuna, sharks, dolphins, whales, seals, and sea turtles, but they are all under threat from pollution, overfishing, and disturbance. Several species may soon become extinct, including the once numerous Mediterranean monk seal.

MEDITERRANEAN MONK SEAL has been reduced to fewer than 400 animals

▲ SUNKEN TREASURE

The Mediterranean civilizations—particularly those of Greece and Rome—are the basis of Western culture. Many relics from these classical cultures have been found in shipwrecks. The earliest finds were dredged up in fishing nets, but when ancient wrecks are located today, they are carefully excavated by marine archeologists.

◄ RED TIDES

Most of the water entering the Mediterranean through the narrow Strait of Gibraltar stays there for about 150 years, becoming more and more polluted with raw sewage and other waste. This causes massive plankton blooms called red tides, especially in the Adriatic. These can be toxic, and their death and decay turns the water stagnant, killing marine life.

▲ BLACK SEA

Linked to the Mediterranean only by the narrow Bosporus, the Black Sea is fed by big rivers such as the Danube and Dneiper that make it less salty than most seas. Soon after the last ice age it was a giant freshwater lake, about 330 ft (100 m) lower than it is now. About 7,000 years ago, however, rising sea levels made water flood in from the Mediterranean, drowning vast areas of land. This may be the origin of the biblical flood story.

Tropical North Atlantic

LIKE MOST OF THE WORLD'S OCEANS, the north Atlantic is swept by a ring of currents that flow in a continuous cycle around the ocean. These currents redistribute heat across the northern hemisphere by carrying warm water north and cool water south, and are exploited by wide-ranging oceanic animals. In the days of sailing ship, the currents and their associated wind systems dictated the routes used by ocean explorers and traders as they traveled the world.

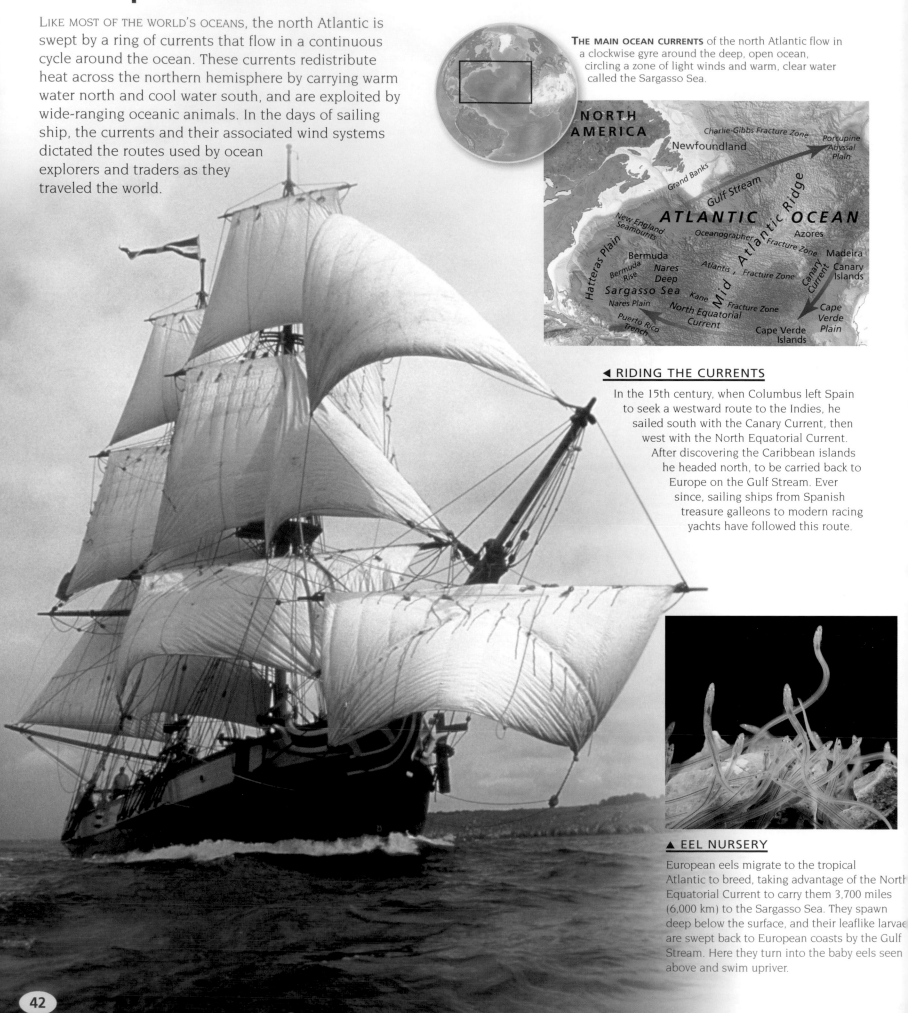

THE MAIN OCEAN CURRENTS of the north Atlantic flow in a clockwise gyre around the deep, open ocean, circling a zone of light winds and warm, clear water called the Sargasso Sea.

NORTH AMERICA

Charlie-Gibbs Fracture Zone
Porcupine Abyssal Plain
Newfoundland
Grand Banks
Gulf Stream
ATLANTIC OCEAN
New England Seamounts
Oceanographer Fracture Zone
Azores
Mid Atlantic Ridge
Hatteras Plain
Bermuda
Bermuda Rise
Nares Deep
Atlantis Fracture Zone
Madeira
Canary Islands
Sargasso Sea
Kane Fracture Zone
Canary Current
Nares Plain
North Equatorial Current
Puerto Rico Trench
Cape Verde Islands
Cape Verde Plain

◀ RIDING THE CURRENTS

In the 15th century, when Columbus left Spain to seek a westward route to the Indies, he sailed south with the Canary Current, then west with the North Equatorial Current. After discovering the Caribbean islands he headed north, to be carried back to Europe on the Gulf Stream. Ever since, sailing ships from Spanish treasure galleons to modern racing yachts have followed this route.

▲ EEL NURSERY

European eels migrate to the tropical Atlantic to breed, taking advantage of the North Equatorial Current to carry them 3,700 miles (6,000 km) to the Sargasso Sea. They spawn deep below the surface, and their leaflike larvae are swept back to European coasts by the Gulf Stream. Here they turn into the baby eels seen above and swim upriver.

SLEEK, STREAMLINED BODY can be propelled through the water with minimal effort

◄ BLUE-WATER HUNTERS

Deep, clear blue tropical waters are so poor in nutrients that there is little plankton, so plankton-eating fish are scarce. Oceanic hunters like tuna, marlin, and dolphins must range widely to find prey, so they have evolved ways of moving at high speed. Species like this marlin are among the fastest of all fish, able to swim at 50 mph (80 km/h) or more.

LONG, SHARP BILL pierces the water to open a channel for the fast-moving fish

EFFICIENT GILLS deliver extra oxygen to the marlin's muscles as it swims faster

FLOATING SEAWEED provides a habitat for eels and other creatures

◄ SARGASSO SEA

The calm zone at the center of the north Atlantic current gyre is occupied by a pool of warm, salty, exceptionally clear water. The surface is covered with floating seaweed that has been concentrated here by circulating currents, but the water below the weed is virtually sterile because it contains hardly any of the vital nutrients that support marine plankton.

NORTH AMERICA

ATLANTIC OCEAN

Sargasso Sea

Caribbean Sea

SOUTH AMERICA

OCEANIC CURRENTS tend to push the weed toward the center of the Sargasso Sea

FLOATING WEED ►

The shallow layer of floating seaweed on the surface of the Sargasso Sea is the main source of food in these clear tropical waters. It is the home of sea turtles and the strange sargassum fish, which is often very difficult to see among the weed because of its superb camouflage. The weed also makes an ideal floating nursery for flying fish, which attach their strings of eggs to the floating fronds as they are carried past the Caribbean on the currents.

SARGASSUM FISH hides amongst the seaweed

DID YOU KNOW?

▸ The converging currents around the Sargasso Sea have heaped its water up into a low mound, a yard (or meter) or so above the level of the surrounding ocean. This feature is also found in the center of other current gyres.

Caribbean

THE OCEAN CURRENTS that swirl westward through the tropical North Atlantic flow through the Caribbean Sea and the islands of the West Indies. This is a region of tropical warmth, glorious blue water, and magical white coral beaches. But it is regularly swept by hurricanes in summer and fall, and these seem to be getting more frequent and more violent as ocean temperatures rise. The clear tropical waters and coral reefs of the Caribbean are also suffering from pollution and disturbance, much of it caused by poorly planned coastal tourist developments. Marine life is suffering as a result, and one local species, the Caribbean monk seal, is now extinct.

THE CARIBBEAN is cut off from the Atlantic by the islands of the West Indies, many of which were formed by volcanoes erupting from the plate boundary marked by the Puerto Rico Trench.

◀ VOLCANIC ISLANDS

The Puerto Rico Trench that curves around the northeast edge of the Caribbean has been created by the Atlantic floor sliding beneath the Caribbean plate. This has also caused the eruption of an island arc of volcanoes on the western side of the trench, above the subduction zone. Many of the volcanoes are dormant, but in July 1995 the eruption of Soufrière Hills on Montserrat destroyed the capital of the island.

▲ HURRICANE ZONE

For much of the year the Caribbean enjoys steady, gentle northeasterly trade winds. But in summer, high sea temperatures in the Atlantic lead to the buildup of tropical oceanic storms that often develop into hurricanes. These are carried westward into the Caribbean, growing stronger all the time and devastating any islands that lie in their path.

SCARLET IBIS glow vivid red among the glossy green foliage of coastal mangroves in Venezuela

◀ MANGROVE FORESTS

Long stretches of Caribbean coastline are fringed with mangrove forests, which grow on the tidal mud. These provide impenetrable refuge for wildlife and vital protection from the storm surge floods generated by hurricanes.

▲ FRINGING REEFS

Coral reefs fringe most of the islands in the Caribbean, and the 160-mile (260-km) Belize Barrier Reef seen here is the second largest coral reef in the world. Built up over centuries from the limestone skeletons of millions of tiny colonial animals, the reef supports at least a thousand species of fish and other marine organisms.

DID YOU KNOW?

▶ The Panama Canal project cost the lives of 27,500 workers. Most of these died from malaria and yellow fever, which were finally controlled by eradicating disease-carrying mosquitoes.

OCEAN-GOING SHIPS can use the canal, although some modern ships are too big to pass through its three sets of locks.

◄ PANAMA CANAL

Opened in 1914 after a long, difficult construction project, the 48-mile (77-km) Panama Canal cuts through a narrow strip of land to link the Pacific Ocean with the Caribbean and the Atlantic. Before the canal was built, ships had to make the notoriously stormy, dangerous passage around Cape Horn at the southern tip of South America.

◄ TURTLE BEACHES

Many species of sea turtles breed on remote beaches in the Caribbean. They bury their eggs in the sand and rely on the tropical warmth to incubate them. Eventually the eggs hatch and the young turtles make their way to the sea. But many beaches are raided by egg-collectors or disturbed by tourists, and turtle numbers are dwindling.

STRONG FLIPPERS help this giant leatherback turtle haul herself over a breeding beach in Trinidad

Gulf of Mexico

ALMOST SURROUNDED BY LAND and shallow shelf seas, the deep basin of the Gulf of Mexico is partly divided by an immense submarine fan of sediment deposited by the Mississippi. The shelf seas contain huge reserves of oil and gas that are vital to the energy-hungry economy of the United States to the north, but the oil industry causes serious pollution problems in this virtually landlocked sea. Most of the Gulf coast is very low-lying and fringed with swamps like the Florida Everglades. The Gulf shores of Mexico and Texas in particular are lined with large lagoons, separated from the sea by barrier beaches. The swampy shores are havens for wildlife, but are regularly flooded by storm surges caused by the hurricanes that sweep the region each summer.

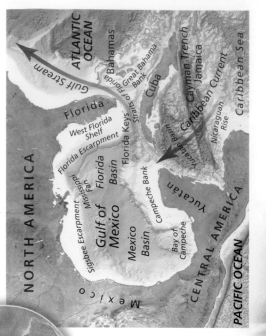

THE GULF OF MEXICO is like a giant bay, cut off from the Caribbean and Atlantic by shallow sills linking Florida, Cuba, and the Yucatán. Water flows in with the Caribbean Current and swirls around the Gulf before leaving in the Gulf Stream.

SWIRLING SEDIMENTS are carried into the Gulf by the waters of the Mississippi

▲ MISSISSIPPI FAN

The mighty Mississippi River carries a huge volume of sand and silt off the heartlands of the United States. This has spilled into the Gulf of Mexico to form an enormous submarine fan covering an area the size of Louisiana and heavy enough to distort the crust of the Earth. Its landward side is capped with a branching delta that extends far out into the Gulf.

SLOW-MOVING MANATEES are air-breathing mammals that feed on floating and submerged vegetation

SWAMPY SHORES ▶

Many Gulf coasts have long sandy beaches backed by marshlands and cypress swamps, and fringed by mangroves, seagrass beds, and chains of low-lying coral islands. The swamps are haunted by alligators and crocodiles, and by water birds such as pelicans, flamingos, and spoonbills. Manatees feed among the seagrass beds, and sea turtles lay their eggs on the more remote beaches.

▲ GULF OIL

The oil and gas reserves that lie beneath the broad continental shelves and slopes to north and south of the Gulf are tapped by more than 800 offshore oil and gas rigs. They have a good safety record, but accidents such as leaks and spills are inevitable. In 1980 a single oil well blowout from the *Ixtoc I* rig in the Bay of Campeche, Mexico, poured 525,000 tons (475,000 metric tons) of oil into the Gulf.

DID YOU KNOW?

Fertilizers carried into the Gulf of Mexico by the Mississippi have caused so much pollution that each summer the deep water south of the delta becomes a giant, oxygen-starved "dead zone" covering 8,500 sq miles (22,000 sq km) or more.

ATLANTIC OCEAN

Cape Canaveral

Miami ●

The *Everglades*

FLORIDA

Jacksonville ●

Tampa ●

Key West ●

Florida Keys

GEORGIA

ALABAMA

MISSISSIPPI

LOUISIANA

Pensacola ●

Mobile ●

New Orleans ●

Mississippi Delta

Gulf of Mexico

Most of southern Florida is low-lying swamp, which would disappear beneath the waves.

Cities such as New Orleans have been built on land that is steadily sinking as fast as sea levels rise and may be uninhabitable by the end of the 21st century.

KEY

CURRENT SEA LEVEL

30 FT (10 M) RISE

UNDER THREAT

Much of the Gulf coast is very low-lying and vulnerable to flooding by hurricanes and rising sea levels. If climate change ever leads to a major meltdown of polar ice, sea levels could rise by over 30 ft (10 m) and huge areas of coastline would be submerged. Even a small rise in sea level could flood many coastal cities.

STORM SURGES will get higher as global climate change makes sea levels rise. The catastrophic flooding caused by Hurricane Katrina in 2005 could soon become an annual event.

COASTAL DEVELOPMENT in areas like Miami—seen here in a satellite image—has swept away the natural flood defenses. The many people who live here are in the front line of any hurricane strike.

MANGROVE SWAMPS like those of the coastal Everglades form natural barriers that absorb the energy of storm waves. They soon recover from hurricanes, but could be submerged by rising sea levels.

West African Seas

THE SOUTH ATLANTIC SURFACE CURRENTS flow counterclockwise, drawing the cold Benguela Current north from the Southern Ocean and through West African seas. The flow then veers west to become the South Equatorial Current. Surface water is drawn offshore to form a fertile upwelling zone off southwest Africa, with abundant plankton that attract shoaling fish and their predators. The cold current also has a strange effect on the climate, creating the foggy Namib desert.

THE MID-ATLANTIC RIDGE snakes through the south Atlantic, its line echoing that of the western edge of Africa, where the rift that grew into an ocean opened up 150 million years ago.

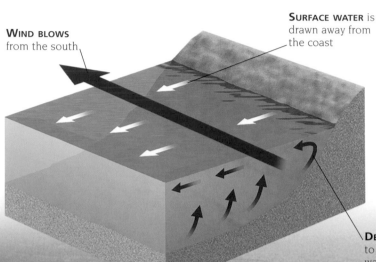

WIND BLOWS from the south

SURFACE WATER is drawn away from the coast

DEEP WATER wells up to replace surface water moving offshore

◄ UPWELLING ZONE

Surface water is driven away from the southwest coast of Africa by a combination of the Earth's rotation and winds blowing from the south. This draws nutrient-rich water up from the shallow continental shelf, fueling the growth of plankton that supports a mass of marine life.

SKELETON COAST ►

Warm, moist air sweeping off the Atlantic toward southwest Africa passes over the cold Benguela Current, and the chill turns the water vapor in the air to fog and rain. By the time the air reaches the Skeleton Coast of Namibia it has lost most of its moisture, and the land is a barren, sandy desert.

Marie Tharp and Bruce Heezen

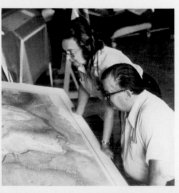

Marie Tharp (1920–2006) was working as assistant to marine geologist Bruce Heezen (1924–1977) when she discovered the rift in the Mid-Atlantic Ridge in 1952. The pair went on to create the first detailed global 3-D map of the ocean floors—a project that took 25 years to complete.

SHARK ATTACK ▼

Big shoals of fish that feed in the ocean off the southern tip of Africa are hunted by Cape fur seals and African penguins. These in turn attract great white sharks, notorious for their ferocity and razor teeth. Some of these sharks have developed a spectacular hunting technique, leaping right out of the water as they slice into their prey.

DEEP DIVER ▶

The deep waters of this region are visited by all the great whales that feed in southern oceans. They include the sperm whale, which regularly dives to depths of over 3,000 ft (1,000 m) to prey on giant squid in the twilight zone. It may be an hour or more before a diving sperm whale returns to the surface for a breath of air.

HUGE HEAD of the sperm whale makes it instantly recognizable

SLAVE SHIPS ▶

In the 17th and 18th centuries, the coasts of West Africa were the main source of the slaves carried across the Atlantic to work on the sugar and cotton plantations of the Caribbean and the Americas. Captured by local slavers, they were sold to European traders and loaded into ships with very little food and water and no sanitation. Conditions were so bad that up to a third might die on the voyage.

DIAMOND SHORES ▼

Some of the world's finest diamonds are found on the shores of southwest Africa. Carried off the continent by ancient rivers, the gemstones are concentrated in coastal gravels by wave action. The coast of Namibia is so rich in these diamonds that they account for nearly half the nation's income.

GLITTERING GEMS are created by cutting the rough stones

CARGO PLAN shows how tightly the slaves were packed together

49

The Chagos-Laccadive Plateau is one of many shallow oceanic plateaus, mostly formed by chains of submarine volcanoes.

The midocean ridge extends south from the Red Sea and splits into southeast and southwest branches.

This 3-D map of the Indian Ocean shows the main features of the ocean floor. The height of these features has been exaggerated to make them easier to see.

ASIA

Himalayas

Tibet

China

The Gulf

Gulf of Oman

Red Sea

Gulf of Aden

Great Rift Valley

Murray Ridge

Arabian Sea

Bay of Bengal

India

Andaman Islands

AFRICA

Owen Fracture Zone

Arabian Basin

Gulf of Thailand

Sri Lanka

South China Sea

Carlsberg Ridge

Chagos-Laccadive Plateau

Maldives

Ceylon Plain

Indones

Somali Basin

Mid-Indian Ridge

Chagos Trench

Sumatra

Sunda Shelf

Seychelles

Mid-Indian Basin

Cocos Basin

Java Trench

Mozambique Channel

Comoros

Mascarene Plateau

INDIAN OCEAN

Investigator Ridge

Christmas Island

Mascarene Basin

North Austra Basin

Mascarene Plain

West Australian Basin

Mauritius

Réunion

Madagascar

Ninetyeast Ridge

Exmou Platea

Cuvier Plateau

Madagascar Basin

East Indiaman Ridge

Mid-Indian Ridge

Perth Basin

Madagascar Plateau

Southwest Indian Ridge

Broken Ridge

Natal Basin

Diamantina Fracture Zone

Agulhas Plateau

Amsterdam Island

South Australian Basin

Crozet Basin

Île St-Paul

Crozet Plateau

Kerguelen Plateau

Southeast Indian Ridge

Southeast Indian Basin

Conrad Rise

Enderby Plain

Davis Sea

ANTARCTICA

Indian Ocean

THE INDIAN OCEAN HAS FORMED over the last 120 million years as India and Australia have gradually drifted away from Africa and Antarctica. The ocean floor has expanded from a midocean ridge shaped like a giant inverted "Y," with its tail extending into the rift that is opening up the Red Sea. The expansion of the ocean has driven India into China, creating the massive crumple zone of the Himalayas and Tibet. Meanwhile the ocean floor is being dragged beneath Indonesia, creating the deep Java Trench and the Sunda Arc of volcanic islands. The warm coastal waters are rich in marine life, but the northern shores of the ocean often suffer from violent, destructive tropical storms.

Widespread flooding makes thousands homeless in Bangladesh each year.

56–57 BAY OF BENGAL

The ocean to the east of India is surrounded by land on three sides, forming the funnel-shaped Bay of Bengal. The low-lying land to the north is regularly swamped by floods as tropical storms sweep in from the sea. The region was badly hit by the 2004 Asian Tsunami.

52–53 MOZAMBIQUE CHANNEL

The southwest Indian Ocean off southern Africa is notorious for dangerous sea conditions created by its strong currents and storm-force winds. But farther north is a region of magical isolated islands with unique wildlife and peaceful shores with small coastal settlements that still rely on traditional fishing as their main source of food.

"Rogue waves" have been blamed for the loss of big ships off South Africa.

Krakatau is one of more than 70 volcanoes in the Sunda Arc.

58–59 THE SUNDA ARC

The elongated islands of Sumatra and Java form the backbone of the Sunda Arc—a chain of volcanoes that mark the boundary where the Indian Ocean floor is plunging beneath Indonesia. This is one of the most volcanically active regions on Earth, and it is regularly shaken by earthquakes and the oceanic tsunamis that they cause.

54–55 ARABIAN SEAS

The seas off Arabia and western India support much more marine life than the open ocean, with food-rich coastal waters and spectacular coral reefs. They are also a major shipping route for oil tankers from the Middle East.

The Suez Canal offers ships an easy passage from the Mediterranean to the Indian Ocean.

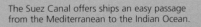

Java Sea

Banda Sea

Arafura Shelf

AUSTRALIA

Mozambique Channel

IN THE SOUTHWEST INDIAN OCEAN, the westward-flowing South Equatorial Current swerves south past the big island of Madagascar and through the Mozambique Channel. Part of the flow then heads west as the Agulhas Current, creating dangerous seas where it encounters storm waves off South Africa. The continental shelf is unusually narrow along much of this coast, and the deep, tropical waters just offshore do not support the dense plankton and big fish shoals found in most shallow seas. But several islands in the region—including Mauritius, Réunion, the Seychelles, and Madagascar itself—are famous for their unique wildlife.

DEEP OCEAN WATER surrounds the island of Madagascar, but shallow submarine plateaus break the surface to form scattered islands such as the Comoros and Seychelles.

◀ ISOLATED ISLANDS

The remote islands of the southern Indian Ocean are inhabited by many animals and plants that are found nowhere else in the world. They include the palm tree that produces the coco-de-mer, a giant seed like a double coconut that drifts on ocean currents. Most of the trees grow in just one valley in the Seychelles.

◀ TRADITIONAL FISHING

Aside from a few big centers like Durban, most of the settlements along the east African coast are small villages. Many of the people depend on fish caught by traditional methods that have little impact on marine life. They use nets cast from the shore or lines trailed from small, simple sailing boats.

▼ GIANT RAY

The enormous, winged manta ray cruises through these tropical seas in search of food. It targets plankton swarms, scooping up the tiny animals by swimming through them with its mouth open and sieving them from the water that flows out through its gill slots. It eats so much that it may weigh 2,200 lb (1,000 kg) or more, and its "wings" may span 23 ft (7 m).

UNIQUE THREE-LOBED TAIL is exactly like those of fish that lived before the first dinosaurs

▲ LIVING FOSSIL

A fish accidentally caught off South Africa in 1938 is virtually identical to the fossil remains of fish that lived more than 300 million years ago. Known as the coelacanth, it has leglike fins and is related to the distant ancestors of all reptiles, birds, and mammals. Coelacanths have now been filmed live around the Comoro Islands in the Mozambique Channel and have also been found as far away as Indonesia.

MODIFIED FINS attached to the manta's head help direct the water flow into its mouth when it swims through a plankton swarm

▼ ROGUE WAVES

As the Agulhas Current flows southwest around the southern cape of Africa, it runs into storm waves built up by strong winds blowing to the northeast. The conflict can heap up giant rogue waves up to 65 ft (20 m) high, big enough to overwhelm even large ships, and several have disappeared in this region.

DID YOU KNOW?

▶ The Indian Ocean island of Mauritius was once the home of the dodo, a giant flightless pigeon that was hunted to extinction by about 1700—less than a century after it was discovered by Portuguese sailors.

Arabian Seas

THE DEEP ARABIAN SEA is swept by currents that reverse direction with the seasons. In summer, rising hot air over Asia draws monsoon winds and rain northeast off the ocean and over India. This drives ocean water eastward in the Somali and Monsoon Currents. The strong winds also drag nutrient-rich waters to the surface off the Gulf of Aden, creating dense blooms of plankton. But in winter the ocean is much warmer than the land, and rising warm air over the ocean draws dry winds southwest off Asia, reversing the current flow. The winds stir up the water in the northern and central Arabian Sea, producing more large plankton blooms. In other areas, such as the Red Sea and the Maldives, marine life is concentrated on coral reefs that are among the most beautiful in the world.

THE NORTHWEST INDIAN OCEAN is spreading from the Carlsberg Ridge, pushing India north into Asia. The spreading rift continues through the Gulf of Aden and the Red Sea.

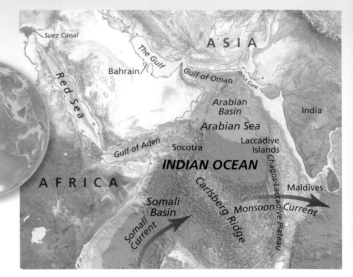

▲ WATER FACTORY

Fresh water is so scarce in the desert states of the Middle East that it has to be made out of seawater. This is done by pumping it through desalination plants that remove the salt. The process is made harder by the fact that the coastal waters are very salty—partly because there is so little rain, and partly because the salt is concentrated as seawater evaporates in the heat.

DAZZLING REEF FISH swim in the clear, warm waters around the corals

◄ RED SEA REEFS

The Red Sea is a rift valley up to 8,000 ft (2,500 m) deep, but it has long, shallow coastal shelves that support spectacular coral reefs. The corals are restricted to these shallow sunlit waters because their survival depends on tiny organisms in their tissues that need sunlight to make food.

◄ HUNGRY GIANTS

The plankton blooms in the Arabian Sea support vast shoals of fish. These provide food for a thriving population of humpback whales, which may stay in the region throughout the year. These whales are feeding by surging upward with their huge mouths open to scoop up fish.

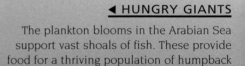

▼ SUEZ CANAL

The Suez Canal links the northwestern tip of the Red Sea with the Mediterranean, enabling ships to pass from European waters into the Indian Ocean without sailing around Africa. The canal took 11 years to build, and 125,000 Egyptian workers died in the process. It has been fought over several times, notably during the Suez Crisis in 1956 when Britain and France, who controlled the canal, tried to prevent its takeover by Egypt.

▲ PERSIAN GULF

The Persian Gulf is much shallower than the Red Sea, but has far fewer coral reefs. It is best known for the huge oil reserves that lie beneath and around it. The oil industry has made the Gulf states rich, but pollution has caused serious problems in the Gulf itself. Wildlife was devastated by the discharge of huge quantities of oil into its waters during the 1991 Gulf War.

UPPER JAW opens to strain hundreds of fish from a single enormous mouthful of water

CORAL REEFS fringing the islands attract thousands of scuba divers to the Maldives, and tourism is now their main industry

CORAL ISLANDS ▶

The 1,196 islands that form the Maldives have been created by coral growing on the shallow Chagos-Laccadive Plateau. Most of the islands are only 3–6 ft (1–2 m) high, and the highest point is just 8 ft (2.4 m) above sea level. This makes them vulnerable to rising sea levels caused by global warming, and many of the islands may soon have to be abandoned.

DID YOU KNOW?

▶ The waters off Bahrain in the Persian Gulf have been famous for pearls since the days of the Assyrians, more than 2,000 years ago. Pearl collecting by traditional breath-holding divers continued until the 1930s.

Bay of Bengal

THE NORTHEAST INDIAN OCEAN forms a huge, roughly triangular bay, with the low-lying land of Bangladesh and the Ganges Delta at its northern tip. The delta is just the cap of the colossal submarine Bengal Fan of sand, silt, and mud that has been carried off the Himalayas by the Ganges, covering 386,000 sq miles (1 million sq km) of sea floor. The low-lying delta region is extremely vulnerable to storm surges that move north up the Bay of Bengal and frequently cause catastrophic flooding. This area was also badly affected by the 2004 Asian Tsunami, which was caused by a submarine earthquake in the deep Java Trench of Sumatra in the Sunda Arc.

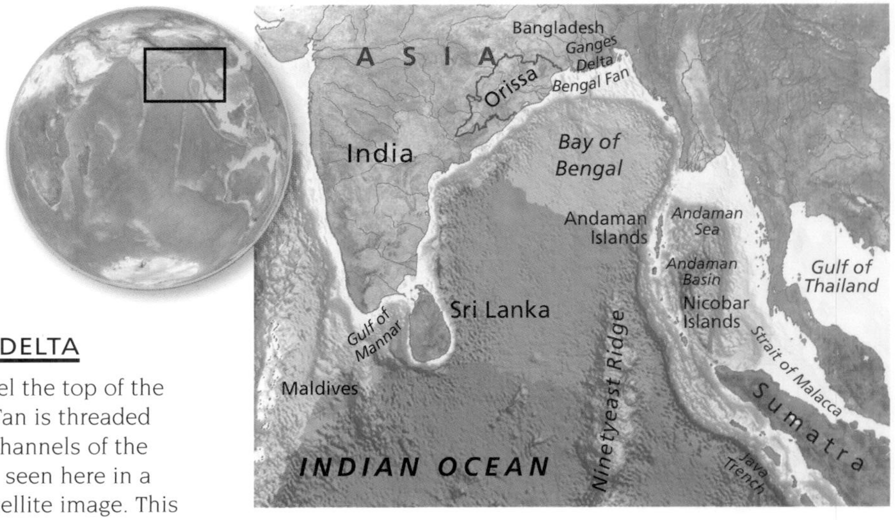

THE BAY OF BENGAL and the Ganges Delta separate India from Southeast Asia. The earthquake zone of the Sunda Arc lies to the east, extending north to the Andaman Islands.

(Map labels: Bangladesh, Ganges Delta, Orissa, Bengal Fan, A S I A, India, Gulf of Mannar, Sri Lanka, Maldives, INDIAN OCEAN, Bay of Bengal, Andaman Islands, Andaman Basin, Andaman Sea, Nicobar Islands, Ninetyeast Ridge, Strait of Malacca, S u m a t r a, Java Trench, Gulf of Thailand)

◀ STORM SURGE

Most of the Ganges Delta region lies close to sea level, and its sea defenses are so poor that a rise in sea level of just 39 in (1 m) could flood 17 percent of Bangladesh. Storm surges caused by tropical cyclones (hurricanes) also have a dramatic effect. In 1999 a storm surge killed more than 10,000 people in the state of Orissa, and in 1970 up to half a million died when a cyclone struck Bangladesh.

◀ GANGES DELTA

Above sea level the top of the huge Bengal Fan is threaded by the many channels of the Ganges Delta, seen here in a false-color satellite image. This also shows vast clouds of river sediment (shown here in purple) being carried out into the Bay of Bengal, where it will eventually settle.

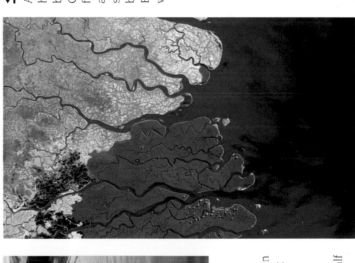

MUDSKIPPERS survive out of the water by carrying a supply of oxygenated water around their gills.

TIDAL SWAMPS ▶

The Ganges Delta has some of the biggest tidal mangrove swamps in the world. Known as the Sundarbans, they provide vital nursery areas for marine fish and refuges for a wonderful variety of animals. These include colorful fiddler crabs, and strange fish called mudskippers that hop around on the mud at low tide.

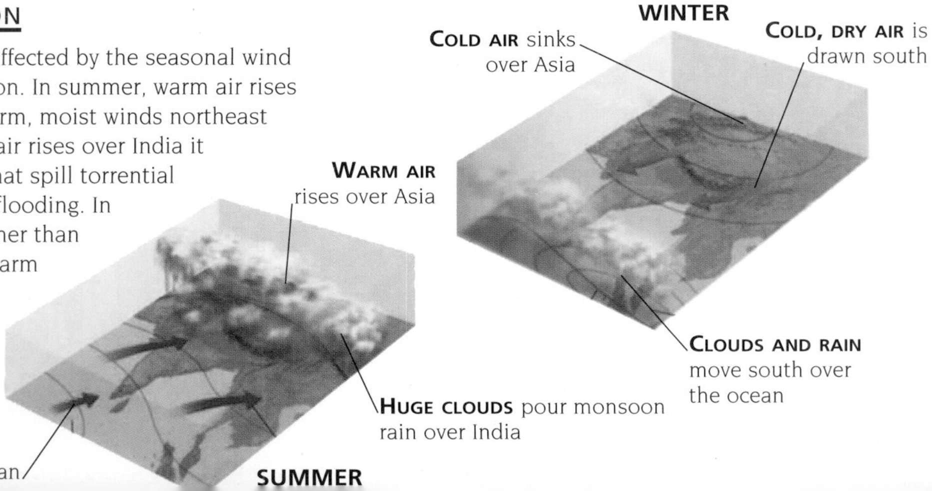

Zheng He

The Chinese admiral Zheng He (1371–1435) was one of the first explorers of the Indian Ocean. He undertook seven voyages in the early 1400s, visiting India, Arabia, and east Africa with a large fleet of at least 60 ships. Some of these were huge vessels, much bigger than European ships of the time.

INDIAN MONSOON

This whole region is affected by the seasonal wind change of the monsoon. In summer, warm air rises over Asia, drawing warm, moist winds northeast off the ocean. As the air rises over India it forms storm clouds that spill torrential rain, causing serious flooding. In winter the sea is warmer than the land, and rising warm air over the ocean draws dry air southwest off Asia, causing droughts.

WINTER

COLD, DRY AIR is drawn south

CLOUDS AND RAIN move south over the ocean

COLD AIR sinks over Asia

WARM AIR rises over Asia

HUGE CLOUDS pour monsoon rain over India

SUMMER

WARM, WET AIR moves in from the ocean

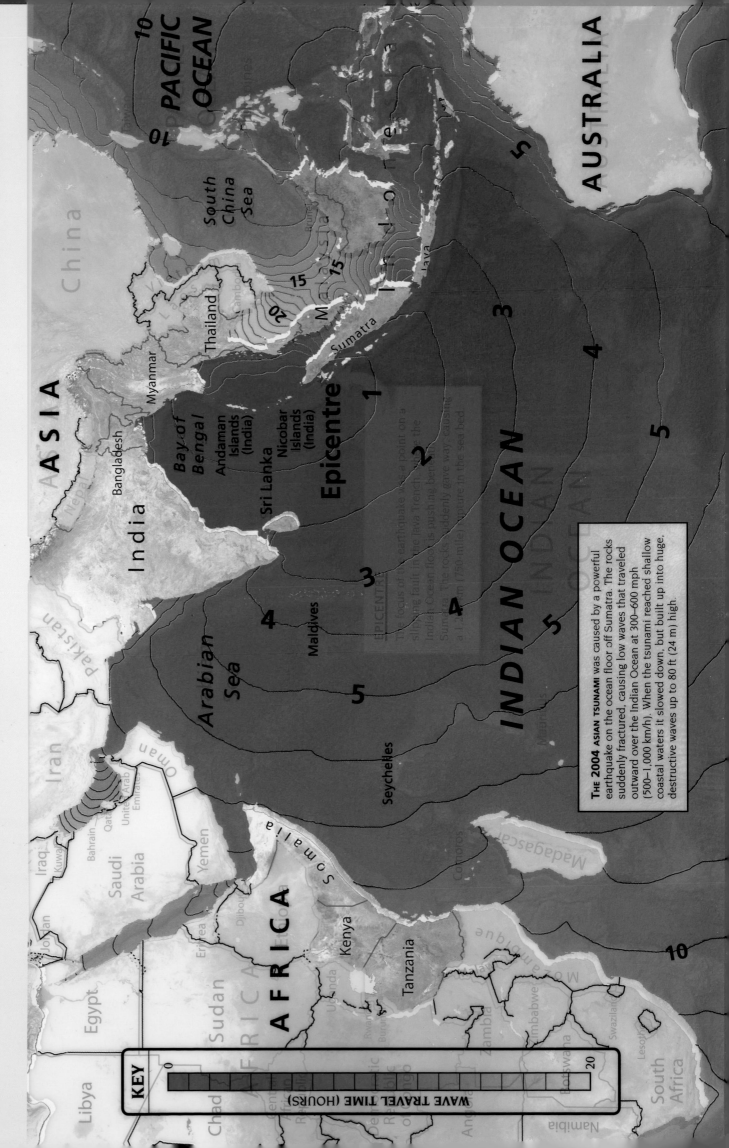

INDIAN OCEAN

PACIFIC OCEAN

ASIA

AUSTRALIA

AFRICA

Epicentre

South China Sea

Bay of Bengal

Arabian Sea

China

India

Pakistan

Iran

Iraq

Kuwait

Bahrain

Qatar

United Arab Emirates

Oman

Yemen

Saudi Arabia

Jordan

Egypt

Sudan

Libya

Chad

Nepal

Bangladesh

Myanmar

Thailand

Sri Lanka

Andaman Islands (India)

Nicobar Islands (India)

Maldives

Seychelles

Sumatra

Java

Malaysia

Eritrea

Djibouti

Somalia

Kenya

Tanzania

Madagascar

Comoros

South Africa

Namibia

Botswana

Lesotho

Swaziland

WAVE TRAVEL TIME (HOURS)

KEY   0   20

THE 2004 ASIAN TSUNAMI was caused by a powerful earthquake on the ocean floor off Sumatra. The rocks suddenly fractured, causing low waves that traveled outward over the Indian Ocean at 300–600 mph (500–1,000 km/h). When the tsunami reached shallow coastal waters it slowed down, but built up into huge, destructive waves up to 80 ft (24 m) high.

EPICENTRE The focus of the earthquake was a point on a slipping fault in the Java Trench — the Indian Ocean floor is pushing beneath Sumatra. The rocks suddenly gave way, causing a 1,200-km (750-mile) rupture in the sea bed

LOW-LYING COASTAL SETTLEMENTS all around the Bay of Bengal were devastated by the 2004 Asian Tsunami. The biggest waves hit the coasts of northern Sumatra, close to the epicentre of the submarine earthquake. This satellite image shows part of this region nearly a year before the tsunami. The land is dotted with settlements and is green with wild and cultivated tropical vegetation. The shallow coastal waters are divided into tidal pools for raising fish and prawns.

THE TSUNAMI STRUCK on 26 December 2004, following the second most powerful earthquake ever measured. This satellite image shows the same area just after the catastrophe. The tidal pools have been swept away by the huge waves, along with nearly all the buildings and green vegetation, and the whole area is covered with brown mud. More than 100,000 people died in Indonesia alone, and nearly 230,000 overall, making it one of the deadliest disasters of the modern era.

The Sunda Arc

INDONESIA HAS BEEN CREATED BY VOLCANOES, including several of the most violent on Earth. They mark the earthquake zone where the floor of the Indian Ocean is plowing beneath Asia, forming the Java Trench and the curved line of volcanoes, known as the Sunda Arc, that extends from northern Sumatra to beyond Timor. The islands have been famous since medieval times for their valuable spices, which were the motive for many early voyages of exploration. The island wildlife is also intriguing, because it is made up of both Asian and Australasian species, brought together as New Guinea and Australia move ever closer to Asia.

THE CURVED LINE OF THE DEEP JAVA TRENCH runs parallel to the line of volcanic islands of the Sunda Arc. The volcanoes shown are just a few of the 70 or more that have erupted in the region since 1900.

◀ EXPLODING ISLANDS

The volcanoes of the Sunda Arc are notorious for their cataclysmic eruptions. In 1815, when Tambora exploded, so much volcanic dust entered the atmosphere there was a "year without a summer" worldwide. In 1883 Krakatau blew itself apart, killing 36,000. Most of Krakatau island disappeared, but in 1927 this new volcano erupted.

SWARMING CRABS follow the same migration routes as their ancestors, regardless of roads, gardens, and even buildings

◀ CRAB INVASION

Christmas Island to the south of Java is the home of millions of red land crabs that live in damp burrows in the tropical rain forests. But every October they are forced to migrate to the coast to spawn, and for two weeks the island is overrun by a red tide of scuttling crabs making their way to the sea.

MAN-EATING CROCODILE ▶

The saltwater crocodile is one of the most powerful of all marine predators. It is the biggest of the crocodiles, estimated to kill about a thousand people a year. It lives mainly among the mangroves that grow on tropical tidal shores, but it often swims long distances between islands. This has enabled it to spread over a huge area, from India to Australia.

STOMACH JUICES are so powerful that the crocodile can digest every scrap of food it eats—even the bones

MACE AND NUTMEG come from the same tree—mace is made from the fruit, while nutmeg is the seed inside

◀ PRECIOUS SPICES

Until the 18th century, the Moluccas and Banda Islands were the only sources of spices such as cloves, mace, and nutmeg. Such spices were—quite literally— worth more than their weight in gold. When the islands were discovered by European adventurers they were bitterly fought over by the Portuguese, Spanish, Dutch, and British. But eventually spice plantations were established in other parts of the tropics, and the so-called Spice Islands were forgotten.

TIDAL POOLS cut out of coastal mangroves are used to raise tiger prawns sold in Western supermarkets

Ferdinand Magellan

The profitable spice trade inspired the first voyage around the world in 1519–1523, when Portuguese explorer Ferdinand Magellan reached them by crossing the Pacific. After he was killed in the Moluccas, his crew returned to Europe via the Indian Ocean.

◀ PRAWN POOLS

Much of the coastline in this region is lined by dense tidal mangrove forest. Large areas of these mangroves have been cleared to make way for tidal pools used for fish and prawn farming, especially on the quieter coasts of the Sunda Shelf. But this eliminates the breeding habitats of many sea fish, and it can weaken or even destroy the living barriers of mangroves protecting the land from storm waves and tsunamis.

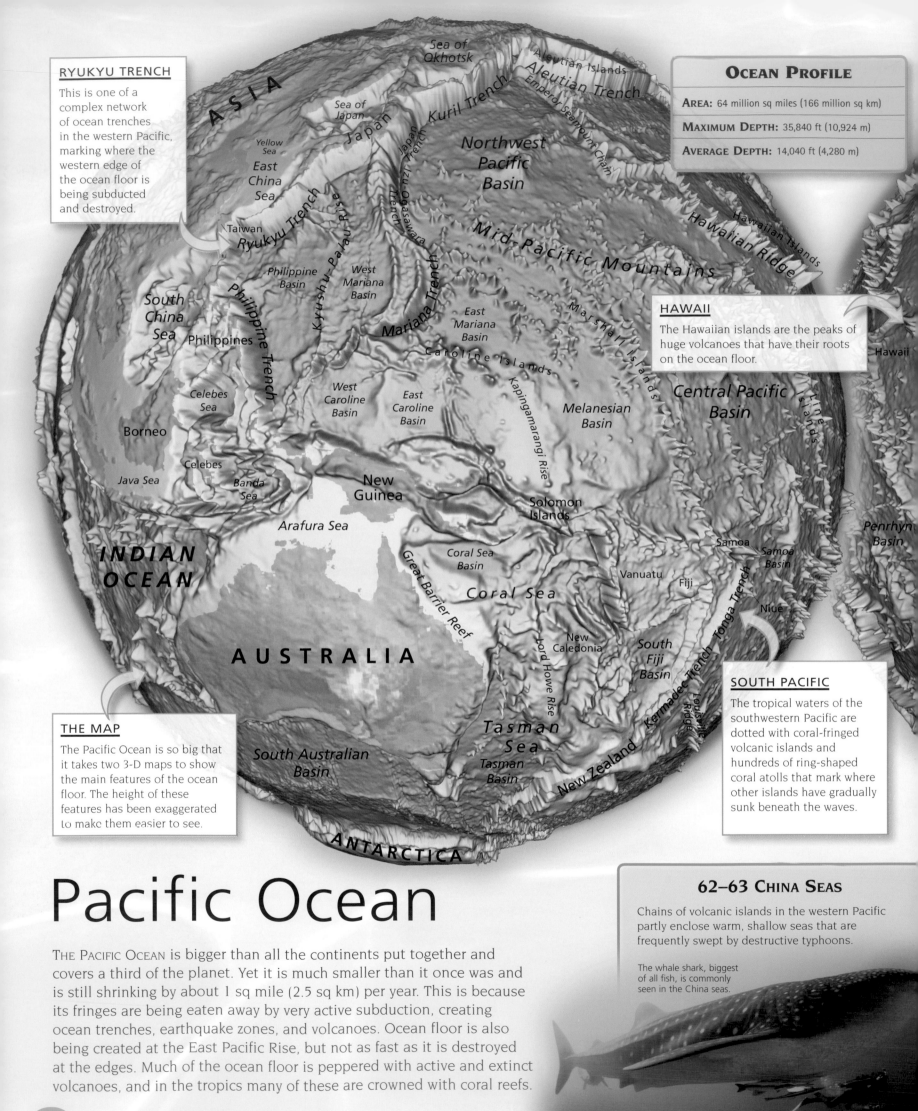

RYUKYU TRENCH

This is one of a complex network of ocean trenches in the western Pacific, marking where the western edge of the ocean floor is being subducted and destroyed.

OCEAN PROFILE

AREA: 64 million sq miles (166 million sq km)

MAXIMUM DEPTH: 35,840 ft (10,924 m)

AVERAGE DEPTH: 14,040 ft (4,280 m)

ASIA

Sea of Okhotsk

Aleutian Islands

Aleutian Trench

Emperor Seamount Chain

Sea of Japan

Kuril Trench

Japan

Yellow Sea

East China Sea

Japan Trench

Japan-Ogasawara Trench

Izu-Ogasawara Trench

Kyushu-Palau Rise

Ryukyu Trench

Taiwan

Northwest Pacific Basin

Mid-Pacific Mountains

Hawaiian Ridge

Hawaiian Islands

South China Sea

Philippine Basin

Philippines

Philippine Trench

West Mariana Basin

Mariana Trench

East Mariana Basin

Caroline Islands

Marshall Islands

HAWAII

The Hawaiian islands are the peaks of huge volcanoes that have their roots on the ocean floor.

Hawaii

Celebes Sea

Borneo

West Caroline Basin

East Caroline Basin

Kapingamarangi Rise

Melanesian Basin

Central Pacific Basin

Line Islands

Java Sea

Celebes

Banda Sea

New Guinea

Solomon Islands

Penrhyn Basin

Arafura Sea

Coral Sea Basin

Samoa

Samoa Basin

INDIAN OCEAN

Vanuatu

Fiji

Coral Sea

Niue

Great Barrier Reef

Lord Howe Rise

New Caledonia

South Fiji Basin

Kermadec Trench

Tonga Trench

Louisville Ridge

SOUTH PACIFIC

The tropical waters of the southwestern Pacific are dotted with coral-fringed volcanic islands and hundreds of ring-shaped coral atolls that mark where other islands have gradually sunk beneath the waves.

AUSTRALIA

South Australian Basin

Tasman Sea

Tasman Basin

New Zealand

THE MAP

The Pacific Ocean is so big that it takes two 3-D maps to show the main features of the ocean floor. The height of these features has been exaggerated to make them easier to see.

ANTARCTICA

Pacific Ocean

THE PACIFIC OCEAN is bigger than all the continents put together and covers a third of the planet. Yet it is much smaller than it once was and is still shrinking by about 1 sq mile (2.5 sq km) per year. This is because its fringes are being eaten away by very active subduction, creating ocean trenches, earthquake zones, and volcanoes. Ocean floor is also being created at the East Pacific Rise, but not as fast as it is destroyed at the edges. Much of the ocean floor is peppered with active and extinct volcanoes, and in the tropics many of these are crowned with coral reefs.

62–63 CHINA SEAS

Chains of volcanic islands in the western Pacific partly enclose warm, shallow seas that are frequently swept by destructive typhoons.

The whale shark, biggest of all fish, is commonly seen in the China seas.

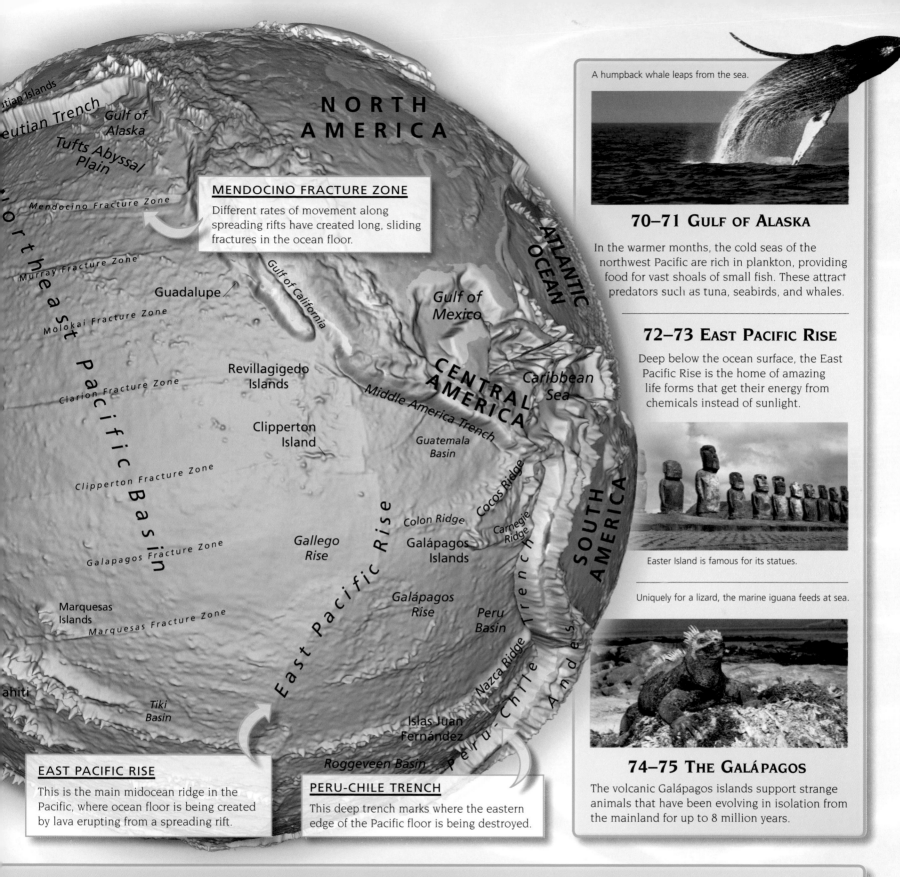

NORTH AMERICA

Aleutian Islands

Aleutian Trench

Gulf of Alaska

Tufts Abyssal Plain

Mendocino Fracture Zone

MENDOCINO FRACTURE ZONE
Different rates of movement along spreading rifts have created long, sliding fractures in the ocean floor.

Northeast Pacific Basin

Murray Fracture Zone

Guadalupe

Gulf of California

Molokai Fracture Zone

Clarion Fracture Zone

Revillagigedo Islands

Clipperton Island

Clipperton Fracture Zone

Galapagos Fracture Zone

Gallego Rise

Marquesas Islands

Marquesas Fracture Zone

East Pacific Rise

Tahiti

Tiki Basin

ATLANTIC OCEAN

Gulf of Mexico

CENTRAL AMERICA

Caribbean Sea

Middle America Trench

Guatemala Basin

Cocos Ridge

Colon Ridge

Carnegie Ridge

Galápagos Islands

Galápagos Rise

Peru Basin

SOUTH AMERICA

Nazca Ridge

Peru-Chile Trench

Andes

Islas Juan Fernández

Roggeveen Basin

EAST PACIFIC RISE
This is the main midocean ridge in the Pacific, where ocean floor is being created by lava erupting from a spreading rift.

PERU-CHILE TRENCH
This deep trench marks where the eastern edge of the Pacific floor is being destroyed.

A humpback whale leaps from the sea.

70–71 GULF OF ALASKA
In the warmer months, the cold seas of the northwest Pacific are rich in plankton, providing food for vast shoals of small fish. These attract predators such as tuna, seabirds, and whales.

72–73 EAST PACIFIC RISE
Deep below the ocean surface, the East Pacific Rise is the home of amazing life forms that get their energy from chemicals instead of sunlight.

Easter Island is famous for its statues.

Uniquely for a lizard, the marine iguana feeds at sea.

74–75 THE GALÁPAGOS
The volcanic Galápagos islands support strange animals that have been evolving in isolation from the mainland for up to 8 million years.

The reef has been built up by at least 400 species of coral.

64–65 GREAT BARRIER REEF
The biggest of all coral reefs lies along the northeastern coast of Australia. It is home to the richest diversity of marine life on the planet.

66–67 OCEANIA
The south Pacific is a vast archipelago of coral islands, formed around the peaks of volcanoes that have erupted from the ocean floor.

The tree-climbing robber crab is found throughout Oceania.

Huge waves roll in from the Pacific and break on Hawaii's shores.

68–69 HAWAII
Isolated in the middle of the Pacific, the islands of Hawaii mark the site of a volcanic "hotspot" beneath the crust of the Pacific Plate.

China Seas

THE WESTERN PACIFIC OFF CHINA AND SOUTHEAST ASIA is divided into several seas separated by chains of islands. These are "island arcs," formed by volcanoes erupting from the ocean floor along boundaries between plates of the Earth's crust. They follow the lines of ocean trenches, where ocean floor is being dragged deep into subduction zones and destroyed. As the crust sinks, friction melts the rock, which then boils up through fissures as molten lava and causes irregular volcanic eruptions. The locking and sudden fracture of the moving plates causes frequent earthquakes and tsunamis.

THE OCEAN FLOOR SOUTH OF JAPAN is pitted with deep trenches, created by subduction zones around the oceanic Philippine Plate. By contrast, most of China's coastal seas lie on the Asian continental shelf.

◀ MARIANA TRENCH

The deepest part of the Mariana Trench plunges to over 36,000 ft (11,000 m) below the waves, making it the deepest chasm on Earth. It lies on the geological frontier where the Pacific Ocean floor is grinding beneath the Philippine Plate, creating both the trench and the matching volcanic island arc of the Mariana Islands.

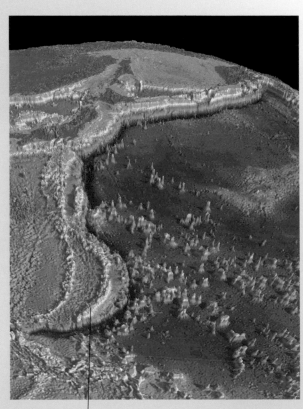

MARIANA ISLANDS follow the curved line of the Mariana Trench, shown in purple on this 3-D image built up from satellite data

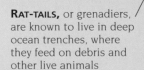

RAT-TAILS, or grenadiers, are known to live in deep ocean trenches, where they feed on debris and other live animals

◀ LIFE IN THE HADAL ZONE

Scientists once believed that animals could not survive in ocean trenches, because of the crushing pressure and intense cold. They called the region the hadal zone, after Hades, the mythical underworld of the dead. But exploration using dredgers, submersibles, and remotely operated vehicles has revealed many creatures living at extreme depths.

WHALE SHARK ▶

The enormous whale shark is frequently seen in the China seas. It is the largest of all fish, capable of growing to a colossal 46 ft (14 m) long. Yet despite its size and its fearsome relatives, it is no threat to people. It feeds only on tiny plankton and small fish, like many whales. Whale sharks cruise widely through the surface waters of tropical oceans in search of concentrations of prey, which they gather by filtering seawater through their sievelike gills.

PALE SPOTS AND BARS form a checkerboard pattern that is unique among sharks

These seas have been important trading routes for centuries, and evidence of this history has been found lying on the seabed. It includes the wreck of the Dutch ship *Geldermalsen*, which sank in the South China Sea on January 3, 1752. The ship was laden with 147 gold bars and 200,000 pieces of porcelain, including this tureen. Discovered in 1985, the porcelain was raised and then auctioned for huge prices as the "Nanking Cargo."

Jacques Piccard

On January 23, 1960, divers Jacques Piccard and Don Walsh descended 35,800 ft (10,912 m) to the bottom of the Mariana Trench in *Trieste*, a primitive submersible designed by Piccard's father, Auguste. They stayed just long enough to see a fish on the seabed, proving that life could exist in the deepest part of the ocean.

▲ SHELF SEAS

The Asian continental shelf extends well offshore from China, beneath shallow coastal seas that are rich in marine life, especially bottom-dwelling fish. The Yellow Sea to the north is named for the yellow silt carried into it by rivers flowing off China, especially the Yellow River and the Yangtze. The silt is clearly visible in this satellite image, billowing out into the clear blue water.

Great Barrier Reef

THE BIGGEST CORAL REEF COMPLEX IN THE WORLD, the Great Barrier Reef is the only structure built entirely by nonhuman, living organisms that is visible from the surface of the Moon. It is about 1,430 miles (2,300 km) long and extends from the southern limit of coral growth, near the Tropic of Capricorn, to the Torres Strait in the north. It has existed for more than 2 million years, but its growth has stopped and started several times to create a mosaic of some 2,000 reefs separated by lagoons and channels and dotted with coral islands.

THE GREAT BARRIER REEF lies along the northeast coast of Australia, on the edge of the Coral Sea that extends east to New Caledonia and the Solomon Islands.

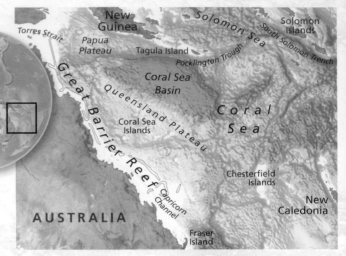

◀ CORAL COLONIES

Reef-building hard corals live in colonies supported by "skeletons" of tough limestone. Living corals have grown on top of dead corals, building up a huge thickness of limestone. The actively growing areas are separated by shallow lagoons, with beds of white coral sand eroded from the reefs by the waves.

TURQUOISE LAGOONS lie between the greenish ridges and patches of living coral

SOLAR ENERGY ▼

The corals that have built the reefs have microscopic organisms called zooxanthellae living in their tissues. These use the energy of sunlight to make sugar out of water and dissolved carbon dioxide—just like the phytoplankton of cooler seas. Corals rely on this process for most of their food, so the reefs grow only in clear, shallow, sunlit water.

◀ GIANT CLAM

Crevices on the reef are often occupied by giant clams, which can grow to 5 ft (1.5 m) across. A giant clam eats planktonic creatures by filtering them from the water that it takes in through its central siphon tube—water that also contains vital oxygen. But it gets a lot of its food in the same way as corals, from tiny zooxanthellae that live under the skin of its colorful "lips" and use the energy of sunlight to make sugar.

RIDGED SHELL
is extremely strong and may keep growing for over 100 years

◀ SERVICE STATION

A small, striped fish called the cleaner wrasse makes a living on the reef by picking parasites and debris from the skin—and even the teeth—of bigger fish. The cleaners always work from particular places on the reef, and other fish visit these "cleaner stations" to enjoy a good grooming. Many of the bigger visitors are fish-eaters, but despite this they rarely attack the cleaners.

DISTINCTIVE STRIPES
probably identify cleaner fish and stop their larger clients from eating them

DEATHLY WHITE ▶

The Great Barrier Reef occasionally suffers from local "plagues" of coral-eating crown-of-thorns starfish, but the biggest threat to the reef is coral bleaching. This can be caused by periods of unusually high water temperatures, which may be linked to global warming. The heat kills the colorful zooxanthellae living in the corals, so the coral turns white and frequently dies.

Captain Cook

The Great Barrier Reef was unknown to science until 1770, when the English navigator Captain James Cook and his crew sailed up the coast of eastern Australia in their ship *Endeavour*. The ship ran onto the hard, jagged coral rock and nearly sank.

Oceania

THE PACIFIC OCEAN FLOOR is peppered with thousands of volcanoes that form volcanic islands or submerged seamounts. These either erupted along plate boundaries to form island arcs, or were created by isolated hotspots beneath the oceanic crust. Most are now extinct, and they are slowly sinking into the crust under their own weight. In the tropical southwest, the islands are ringed or crowned by coral reefs that support an amazing variety of marine life. By contrast, the islands have few native land animals, and the local people get much of their living from the coral seas.

THE SOUTH PACIFIC is dotted with some 25,000 coral-fringed islands that form the realm of Oceania. Some are volcanic peaks that rise above the waves, but many are just low-lying reefs crowned by a few palm trees.

◄ BIRD ISLANDS

Coral islands make ideal nesting sites for ocean birds such as frigatebirds. These ocean wanderers are famous for catching flying fish, seizing them as they escape from other predators by leaping from the water on their long, winglike fins.

TREE CRAB ►

Although the coral islands have few true land animals, some sea creatures have evolved ways of surviving out of the water. Most impressive is the robber crab, a giant, coconut-eating relative of the hermit crabs that can climb trees.

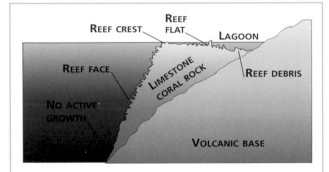

FRINGING REEF

The coral reef surrounding a volcanic island grows on its submerged slopes to form a steep barrier against the ocean. When the volcano becomes extinct and starts to sink under its own weight, the coral keeps growing at the reef crest to enclose a shallow, sheltered lagoon.

RISING SEA LEVELS ►

Global warming is melting the ice on Greenland and Antarctica, and world sea levels are rising as meltwater pours into the oceans. This is catastrophic for many of the low-lying coral nations of Oceania. The people of Tuvalu, north of Fiji, have already made plans to abandon their flooded islands.

REEF FISH of many species feed in the clear water around a broad, spreading plate of staghorn coral

▼ DAZZLING DIVERSITY

There is not much food available on a coral reef. Within each reef community a species has to find a strategy for survival, or move out. This has encouraged the evolution of a wonderful diversity of animals, with few of each species on each reef. By contrast, the richer seas of cooler regions support more animals, but these tend to form big populations of just a few species.

Motu Piti Aau

Motu Tofari

Motu Ome

Motu Moute

Motu Haapiti

Motu Tevairoa

Motu Ahuna

Motu Tapu

THE LAGOON makes a refuge for many animals that prefer shallow, calm waters to the deep, rough seas of the open ocean. The sandy floor of the lagoon conceals clams and other shellfish that are hunted by rays—flattened relatives of sharks that use their winglike fins to "fly" through the sunlit shallows.

SHELTERED BEACHES in the lagoon may be used by sea turtles, which lay their eggs in the sand. Seagrass beds in the shallows are grazed by green turtles and dugongs.

THOUSANDS OF YEARS INTO THE FUTURE, this shallow lagoon will mark the site of the central "high island" of Bora Bora, near Tahiti in the South Pacific. The island was created by a volcano erupting from the floor of the Pacific Ocean about 3 million years ago, but became extinct and gradually started sinking back into the ocean.

LOW ISLANDS on the barrier reef will change their shape over the millions of years that the central island takes to sink. They may grow and eventually join up to form a complete ring around the lagoon.

THE SURROUNDING BARRIER REEF traces the original coastline of the volcanic island before it started to sink. It continues to grow upward as its foundations subside, creating a ring-shaped atoll. Ocean waves break on the outside edge of the reef.

CORAL ATOLLS ▶

Many of the coral islands in the South Pacific are atolls—rings of coral crowned with low banks of sand. Their formation was explained by the naturalist Charles Darwin in the 1840s, who realized that each atoll originates as a fringing reef around a volcanic island. When the volcano becomes extinct the island starts sinking, and the reef grows upward to form a barrier reef around a lagoon with a central island. Eventually the volcanic peak vanishes completely, leaving just a ring of coral around a blue lagoon.

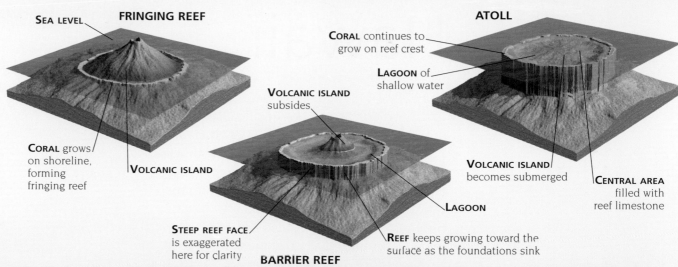

FRINGING REEF

SEA LEVEL

CORAL grows on shoreline, forming fringing reef

VOLCANIC ISLAND

VOLCANIC ISLAND subsides

STEEP REEF FACE is exaggerated here for clarity

BARRIER REEF

LAGOON

REEF keeps growing toward the surface as the foundations sink

ATOLL

CORAL continues to grow on reef crest

LAGOON of shallow water

VOLCANIC ISLAND becomes submerged

CENTRAL AREA filled with reef limestone

A FUTURE ATOLL

The volcanic, coral-fringed island of Bora Bora, Tahiti, will eventually turn into an atoll as the central peak subsides beneath the waves.

SHELTERED LAGOON

The volcanic island is surrounded by a calm lagoon, sheltered from the big waves of the open Pacific by the barrier reef.

VOLCANIC PEAK

The central "high island" of Bora Bora is the peak of an extinct volcano that rises more than 3 miles (5 km) from the floor of the Pacific.

BARRIER REEF

A coral reef has grown up from the original shoreline of the volcano and forms an encircling barrier against the ocean.

MOTU

Low-lying sandy islands called motus cap many parts of the barrier reef.

REEF FLAT

The reef gives way to a bed of coral sand dotted with patches of living coral, which slopes gently into the central lagoon.

Hawaii

THE HAWAIIAN ISLANDS ARE A CHAIN OF VOLCANOES that have erupted as the Pacific Ocean floor moves over a stationary "hotspot" beneath the Earth's crust. The surrounding tropical ocean is very deep and relatively barren, but the islands themselves are fringed by coral reefs that teem with colorful marine life. Submerged seamounts also create local upcurrents that carry nutrients to the surface, creating blooms of plankton that support fish and other animals.

THE HAWAIIAN ISLAND CHAIN forms the southern end of a 3,739-mile- (6,000-km-) long volcanic ridge extending across the floor of the north Pacific.

KAUAI
has been extinct for 5 million years and is sinking each year

MAUI
has moved off the hotspot, and is subsiding

HAWAII
is right over the hotspot and is volcanically highly active

SEAMOUNT CHAIN
of submerged extinct volcanoes extends north

HOTSPOT
in the mantle fuels volcanic eruptions

▲ HOTSPOT

The Pacific plate is slipping northwest over the hotspot at about 4 in (9 cm) a year, and for millions of years the hotspot has been burning a line of volcanoes through the moving plate. The hotspot is currently under Hawaii itself, and the volcanoes on the other islands are now subsiding under their own enormous weight.

BASALT LAVA erupting from Kilauea flows down the volcano toward the sea

◀ FIRE FOUNTAIN

The molten basalt that erupts from Hawaii has formed huge shield volcanoes that rise all the way from the ocean floor, 3 miles (5 km) below sea level. The largest, Mauna Loa, is the biggest volcano on Earth. Kilauea, on the island's southern flank, is the most active and is in virtually constant eruption.

John Tuzo Wilson

The first person in Canada to get a university degree in geophysics, John Tuzo Wilson later developed the hotspot theory of volcanic island chains that explains the formation of the Hawaiian islands and seamounts.

HAWAIIAN SURF ▶

Many of the waves that crash onto the beaches of Hawaii have traveled vast distances across the Pacific from the Southern Ocean, where fierce storms have generated giant waves. When they surge into the shallow water around the islands they shorten and steepen, and may be up to 30 ft (9 m) high when they break. These giant waves make Hawaii a magnet for experienced surfers.

HAMMERHEAD SHARK is one of the many species attracted to seamounts

▼ WILDLIFE HOTSPOTS

Seamounts like those that extend northwest from the Hawaiian islands are submarine volcanoes that rise like mountains from the ocean floor. As ocean currents sweep water up and over these submerged peaks they drag nutrients up with them, creating fertile waters that support plankton, fish, and predators such as sharks.

▲ OCEANIC RAIN

The trade winds that blow from the northeast in the northern tropics pick up moisture from the ocean and dump it on the islands as rain. Most of it falls on the windward side of the mountains, and the northeast flank of Mount Waialeale on Kauai is one of the wettest places in the world, with higher rainfall than the rain forests of Amazonia. By contrast, the leeward slopes are relatively dry and barren.

Gulf of Alaska

IN CONTRAST TO THE WARM CORAL SEAS OF THE TROPICS, the northeast Pacific is a region of storms and cold currents that stir up deep, rich waters. These cause seasonal plankton blooms that support large populations of fish, seabirds, and other animals, and attract migratory humpback, gray, and killer whales. Near the shores, forests of giant seaweed shelter fish and shellfish that are hunted by seals, sea lions, and sea otters. The region is also notorious for its earthquakes, which can cause tsunamis.

THE GULF OF ALASKA is separated from the Bering Sea by the Aleutian islands. The Pacific floor is sliding northwest into the Aleutian Trench, along a fault that passes through California.

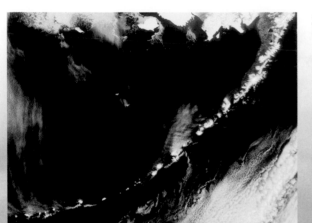

◀ ISLAND ARC

The Aleutian Islands are a long chain of volcanoes that have erupted along the line of the Aleutian Trench, where the Pacific Ocean floor is plunging beneath the Bering Sea and Alaska. They form a perfect arc along the plate boundary to the north of the trench. In this satellite view they are picked out by the white snowfields that have formed on many of the volcanic peaks.

◀ SEASONAL RICHES

Winter storms stir up nutrients that fuel massive plankton blooms in spring. These feed vast shoals of fish and bigger animals like this humpback whale. In summer, a surface layer of warm water prevents nutrients from reaching the surface, and plankton growth slows down until the storms of fall.

DID YOU KNOW?

▶ On Good Friday 1964, Prince William Sound in the Gulf of Alaska was the focus of the most powerful earthquake ever recorded in the US. The Pacific floor slid 65 ft (20 m) beneath Alaska in three minutes, raising parts of the shoreline 33 ft (10 m) into the air. But, luckily, so few people live in the region that only 131 died.

◀ KELP FORESTS

Huge seaweeds known as giant or bull kelp grow near the coastline. Their fronds can grow 2 ft (60 cm) a day to reach heights of 100 ft (30 m) or more. The kelp forests support large numbers of grazing sea urchins, which are hunted by sea otters. Where otters are scarce, the hungry sea urchins often destroy the kelp.

◀ OIL SPILL

In March 1989, the giant oil tanker *Exxon Valdez* ran aground in Prince William Sound, and 12 million gallons (42 million liters) of crude oil leaked into the sea. The oil spill was the most destructive in history, killing more than 250,000 seabirds, up to 6,000 sea otters, 200 harbor seals, and 22 killer whales. Here the oil left in the stricken tanker is being pumped into a smaller ship—part of a clean-up operation that cost at least two billion dollars.

WHALE-WATCHING TOURISTS make special trips to enjoy close encounters with gray whales

SPINY SEA URCHINS make prickly meals, so sea otters smash them open on stones gathered from the seabed

◀ MIGRANT WHALES

The north Pacific gray whale feeds in a unique way—by plowing through the soft bottom sediments in shallow coastal waters to stir up clouds of mud. This exposes small animals, which it then strains from the cloudy water. Many gray whales feed in the Gulf of Alaska in summer, then migrate along the North-American coast to spend the winter in the warmer waters off California and Mexico.

BROWN PELICANS plunge-dive for fish off the Pacific coast

UPWELLING ZONE ▶

Off the northwestern United States, surface water is dragged offshore by ocean currents. Deeper water from just above the continental shelf wells up to replace it, bringing dissolved nutrients to the surface. The nutrients enable plankton to flourish and multiply, providing plenty of food for shoaling fish and seabirds.

East Pacific Rise

THE PACIFIC IS SHRINKING, as its fringes are slowly engulfed in deep ocean trenches. Meanwhile the ocean floor is being ripped apart at the East Pacific Rise. This midocean ridge has many volcanic vents and hot springs known as black smokers, which gush superheated, mineral-rich water into the cold, dark ocean depths. These black smokers support amazing communities of organisms that get all their energy from the chemicals in the water, instead of from sunlight like nearly all other life on Earth.

Map labels:
San Francisco
San Andreas Fault
NORTH AMERICA
Guadalupe
Gulf of California
Gulf of Mexico
Mexico
Revillagigedo Islands
Middle America Trench
PACIFIC OCEAN
Guatemala Basin
Colón Ridge
Cocos Ridge
Panama Basin
Galápagos Islands
Gallego Rise
East Pacific Rise
Bauer Basin
Galápagos Rise
Peru Basin
Pitcairn Islands
Yupanqui Basin
Easter Island
Sala y Gomez
Sala y Gomez Ridge

THE EAST PACIFIC RISE is a spreading rift which extends into the Gulf of California to join the sliding San Andreas Fault

SPREADING RIFT ▶

This 3-D sonar image shows the East Pacific Rise snaking along the ocean floor. Its rift is spreading about ten times faster than the Mid-Atlantic Ridge, at up to 8½ in (22 cm) a year, but it is not as high because the rock underneath is so hot and soft that it cannot support high submarine mountains.

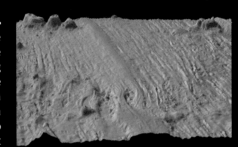

TALL CHIMNEYS, built up from the same minerals that make the gushing water look black, grow up around the hot vents

GIANT TUBEWORMS live around many hydrothermal vents

BLACK SMOKERS ▶

The rift valley along the spine of the ridge is peppered with hydrothermal vents, which gush volcanically heated water from the hot rock. The high pressure at depth stops the water from boiling, so it can reach temperatures of 750°F (400°C). It is full of dissolved minerals that often form black particles, like smoke, when the hot vent water is cooled by contact with the near-freezing ocean.

EASTER ISLAND ▶

The famous statues of Easter Island are made of volcanic rocks that erupted from the East Pacific Rise. The island is made up of three volcanoes that were probably formed by a hotspot beneath the ridge and have since been carried east by movement of the ocean floor.

CUTAWAY VIEW shows superheated water erupting from the vent

◀ GULF OF CALIFORNIA

The rocks on each side of the East Pacific Rise are fractured by long, sliding transform faults. One of these faults has created the Gulf of California, which is a haven for ocean life such as shoaling fish, squid, sharks, sea lions, and whales. The fault line continues northwest under California as the San Andreas Fault, responsible for the many earthquakes that have rocked cities such as San Francisco.

▼ GIANT WORMS

Many black smokers are surrounded by clusters of giant tubeworms, clams, mussels, and swarms of blind white crabs. They all live on microscopic bacteria that gather chemicals from the vent water, mix them with oxygen to release energy, and use this to make food. The crabs eat the bacteria, but the tubeworms, clams, and mussels grow colonies of bacteria inside their bodies and live on the food that they make.

Colleen Cavanaugh

In 1980, Colleen Cavanaugh was in her first year as a graduate student when she discovered how the giant worms were able to live without light—by growing colonies of chemical-processing bacteria inside their own bodies.

RED GILLS of giant tubeworms absorb oxygen and vital chemicals from the water

The Galápagos

THE VOLCANIC ISLANDS OF THE GALÁPAGOS LIE IN THE PATH OF COLD, nutrient-rich ocean currents flowing northwest off Peru. The fertile waters encourage the growth of plankton that support a mass of ocean life, and this provides food for seabirds and many other unique animals. But a seasonal warming of the ocean surface, known as El Niño, often suppresses the food-rich cooler waters, and in bad years the wildlife may starve. El Niño can also disrupt the weather, causing flooding on the Pacific coasts of America and droughts in Australia and Indonesia.

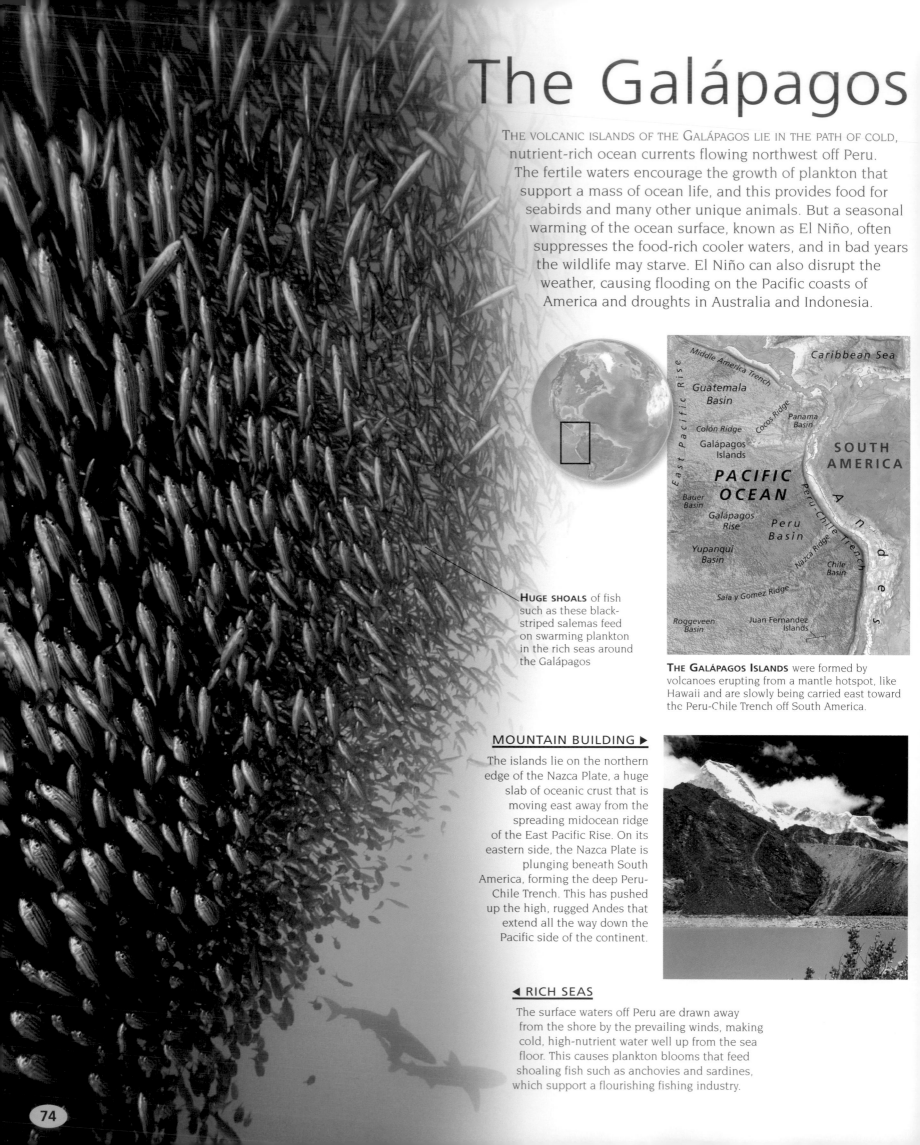

HUGE SHOALS of fish such as these black-striped salemas feed on swarming plankton in the rich seas around the Galápagos

THE GALÁPAGOS ISLANDS were formed by volcanoes erupting from a mantle hotspot, like Hawaii and are slowly being carried east toward the Peru-Chile Trench off South America.

MOUNTAIN BUILDING ▶

The islands lie on the northern edge of the Nazca Plate, a huge slab of oceanic crust that is moving east away from the spreading midocean ridge of the East Pacific Rise. On its eastern side, the Nazca Plate is plunging beneath South America, forming the deep Peru-Chile Trench. This has pushed up the high, rugged Andes that extend all the way down the Pacific side of the continent.

◀ RICH SEAS

The surface waters off Peru are drawn away from the shore by the prevailing winds, making cold, high-nutrient water well up from the sea floor. This causes plankton blooms that feed shoaling fish such as anchovies and sardines, which support a flourishing fishing industry.

GUANO ISLANDS ▶

The big fish shoals feed seabirds such as the guanay cormorant, which breeds in colonies on islands off Peru. The birds have been doing this for so long that their droppings have formed deep deposits, called guano. This is very rich in phosphates and nitrates, which are vital plant nutrients, and in the 19th century the guano was mined for use as fertilizer.

ROCKY ISLAND is covered with a thick, hard layer of guano

GUANAY CORMORANTS once bred in colonies of a million or more

Charles Darwin

Darwin's visit to the Galápagos in 1835 led to his theory of evolution by natural selection. He saw that the animals on different islands had developed in different ways and realized this was because some strains were more likely to survive than others. This idea is known simply as the "survival of the fittest."

SATELLITE IMAGE shows warm surface water in red during an El Niño event

MARINE IGUANA is the only lizard in the world that feeds in the sea

UNIQUE SPECIES ▶

Cut off from the South American mainland by nearly 600 miles (1,000 km) of ocean, the animals of the Galápagos have evolved in their own unique way. They include flightless cormorants, several types of giant tortoises, and strange marine iguanas. The islands are also home to penguins, albatrosses, frigatebirds, fur seals, and sea lions.

▲ EL NIÑO

Every five years or so, a change in the wind pattern over the tropical Pacific weakens the ocean currents that flow from east to west. Warm surface water flows back east, to smother the denser, colder waters that supply nutrients to the marine life of the eastern Pacific. These El Niño events always occur around Christmas and can devastate fish stocks.

SUN-BAKED VOLCANIC ROCK makes an ideal spot for a marine iguana to warm up after a feeding trip in the cold ocean

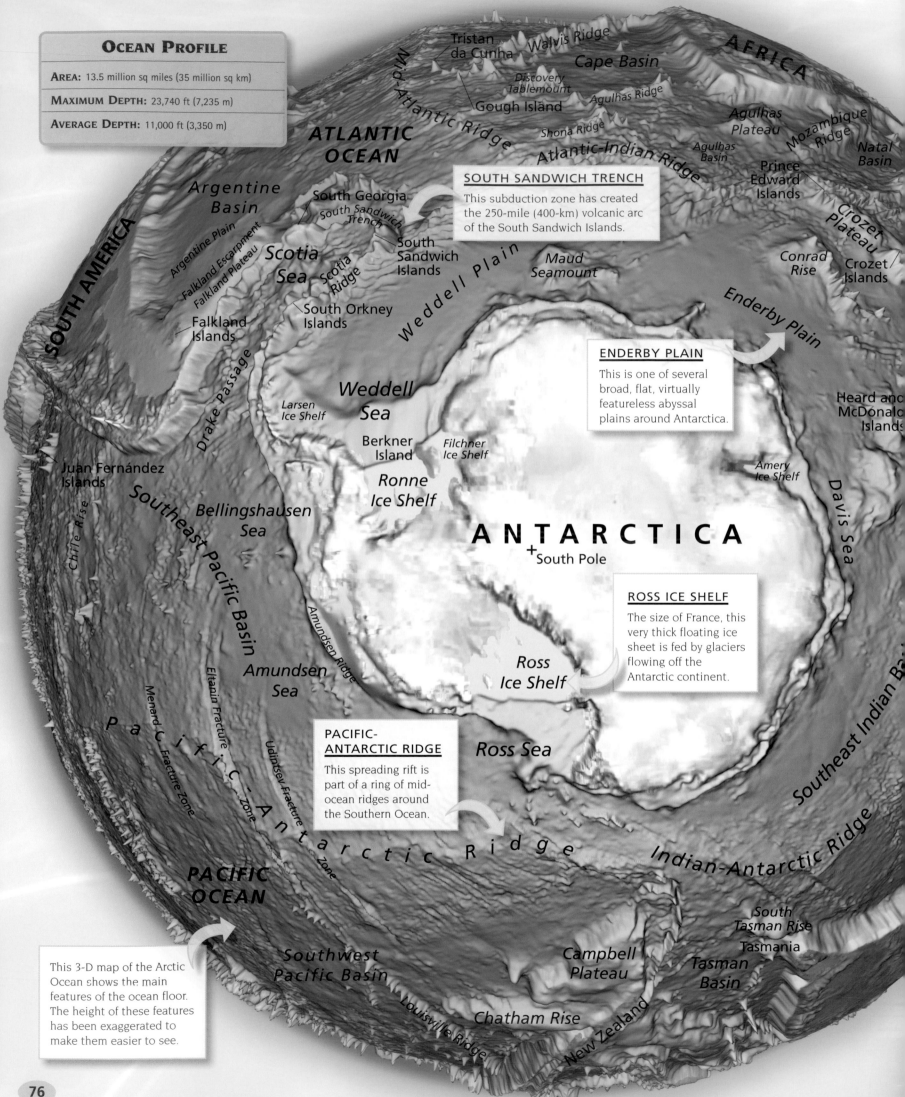

ATLANTIC OCEAN

A F R I C A

Tristan da Cunha

Walvis Ridge

Cape Basin

Discovery Tablemount

Gough Island

Agulhas Ridge

Shona Ridge

Mid-Atlantic Ridge

Atlantic-Indian Ridge

Agulhas Plateau

Mozambique Ridge

Agulhas Basin

Prince Edward Islands

Natal Basin

Crozet Plateau

Argentine Basin

South Georgia

South Sandwich Trench

Scotia Sea

Scotia Ridge

South Sandwich Islands

Conrad Rise

Crozet Islands

SOUTH SANDWICH TRENCH

This subduction zone has created the 250-mile (400-km) volcanic arc of the South Sandwich Islands.

Argentine Plain

Falkland Escarpment

Falkland Plateau

SOUTH AMERICA

Falkland Islands

South Orkney Islands

Weddell Plain

Maud Seamount

Enderby Plain

Drake Passage

Weddell Sea

Larsen Ice Shelf

Berkner Island

Filchner Ice Shelf

Ronne Ice Shelf

ENDERBY PLAIN

This is one of several broad, flat, virtually featureless abyssal plains around Antarctica.

Heard and McDonald Islands

Amery Ice Shelf

Juan Fernández Islands

Bellingshausen Sea

ANTARCTICA

+ South Pole

Davis Sea

Chile Rise

Southeast Pacific Basin

ROSS ICE SHELF

The size of France, this very thick floating ice sheet is fed by glaciers flowing off the Antarctic continent.

Amundsen Ridge

Amundsen Sea

Eltanin Fracture Zone

Menard Fracture Zone

Udintsev Fracture Zone

Ross Ice Shelf

Ross Sea

Southeast Indian Ba

P a c i f i c - A n t a r c t i c   R i d g e

PACIFIC-ANTARCTIC RIDGE

This spreading rift is part of a ring of mid-ocean ridges around the Southern Ocean.

Indian-Antarctic Ridge

PACIFIC OCEAN

Southwest Pacific Basin

Louisville Ridge

Campbell Plateau

Chatham Rise

New Zealand

South Tasman Rise

Tasmania

Tasman Basin

This 3-D map of the Arctic Ocean shows the main features of the ocean floor. The height of these features has been exaggerated to make them easier to see.

Southern Ocean

THE SOUTHERN OCEAN is unlike all the other oceans, because it has no obvious boundaries. Its frontier is the Antarctic Convergence, where the water of the extreme south Pacific, Atlantic, and Indian oceans meets the colder, denser ocean water surrounding Antarctica. Most of this water moves east around the continent, in a current driven by high winds that also heap up huge waves. Closer inshore, a current flowing in the opposite direction carries coastal pack ice steadily westward. In summer, only the seas nearest Antarctica are frozen, but the winter sea ice covers a vast area, extending some 500 miles (800 km) offshore.

thwest
Ridge

ozet

Kerguelen Island

erguelen Plateau

INDIAN OCEAN

theast
dian Ridge

TRALIA

78–79 SUBANTARCTIC ISLANDS

The margins of the Southern Ocean are dotted with remote rocky islands. Although these are largely covered by snow and ice, especially in winter, their coasts thaw out in summer to provide vital breeding grounds for many of the seals and penguins that feed in Antarctic waters, as well as other ocean birds such as albatrosses.

Rival male southern elephant seals fight for control of a breeding beach on the island of South Georgia.

80–81 WEDDELL SEA

Hemmed in to the west by the sinuous curve of the Antarctic Peninsula, the Weddell Sea is a huge bay on the Atlantic flank of Antarctica. Its southern shores lie beneath the enormous Ronne Ice Shelf, and its waters are covered by floating sea ice that forms a drifting mass of ice floes in summer. This area is an important source of the cold deep-water currents that flow north over the ocean floors of the world.

Emperor penguins breed on the floating ice of the Weddell Sea, supporting their eggs on their feet to stop them from freezing solid.

82–83 THE ICY OCEAN

In winter, the sea ice around Antarctica expands into a huge, broken sheet that covers an area far bigger than the continent itself. This transformation dominates the lives of many Antarctic animals, forcing them north to areas where they can still feed in open water.

Vast, flat-topped icebergs break off the Antarctic ice shelves and drift through the Southern Ocean. Some of these tabular icebergs are as big as cities, or even entire US states.

Subantarctic Islands

THE ISLANDS THAT ARE SCATTERED AROUND THE ANTARCTIC FRINGES are isolated rocky outcrops in a rich but violent ocean. They are bleak, cold, windswept places, and almost barren except for the tough tussock grasses that grow on the coastal lowlands. But unlike most of Antarctica they thaw out in summer, providing many of the seals and seabirds of the Southern Ocean with the ice-free sites that they need for breeding. Some of these seasonal breeding colonies are among the largest on Earth, but in winter the islands are virtually deserted.

MANY OF THE SUBANTARCTIC ISLANDS form part of the Scotia Arc, a volcanic island arc with deep ocean trenches in the extreme south Atlantic.

◀ STORMY WATERS

The high winds and steep waves of the Southern Ocean have been notorious since the first ships tried to sail around Cape Horn, at the tip of South America. A sailing ship heading west could take weeks to overcome the contrary winds and currents, and the return passage was almost as bad. Many ships were wrecked or damaged, like the *Lady Elizabeth*, abandoned in the Falkland Islands in 1913.

AUTOMATED INSTRUMENTS collect data throughout the year.

◀ SCIENTIFIC RESEARCH

Since they are the least inhospitable parts of Antarctica, the Subantarctic islands and the northern tip of the Antarctic Peninsula are dotted with many scientific research stations. Many are manned only in summer, when the geology, climate, and wildlife can be studied in virtually continuous daylight.

▼ SCOTIA ARC

The rugged peaks of the South Orkney Islands have been pushed up along the Scotia Arc, a destructive plate boundary linking South America and the Antarctic Peninsula. Mountain-building and volcanic eruptions have created a looping chain of islands from the South Shetlands to South Georgia.

LONG, NARROW WINGS enable the albatross to soar over the ocean like a sailplane

◄ OCEAN WANDERER

The magnificent wandering albatross spends most of its long life riding the winds over the Southern Ocean as it searches for surface-swimming fish and squid. Every two years it returns to its traditional nesting sites on islands such as South Georgia to breed.

GLACIERS flow down the rocky flanks of the mountains toward the sea.

▲ BREEDING COLONIES

Huge colonies of penguins and seals gather on the islands each summer to breed. These male elephant seals are struggling for control of a stretch of beach in South Georgia. Only the victor will get the opportunity to mate with the females on the beach.

KING PENGUINS are dwarfed by the massive bulk of the seals

◄ ANTARCTIC TOURISM

The Antarctic Peninsula and the islands of the Scotia Arc are now regularly visited by cruise ships that offer guided trips ashore and give a unique glimpse of this extreme environment. But tourism is also putting the area under increasing strain, despite the existence of Antarctic treaties designed to prevent the exploitation of the region.

DID YOU KNOW?

▶ Most Antarctic penguins must breed in places where there is no snow, and these can be hard to find. But on the volcanic South Sandwich island of Zavodovski, the heat of the volcano keeps much of the ground snow-free, creating a centrally heated paradise for the million or more pairs of chinstrap penguins that breed there.

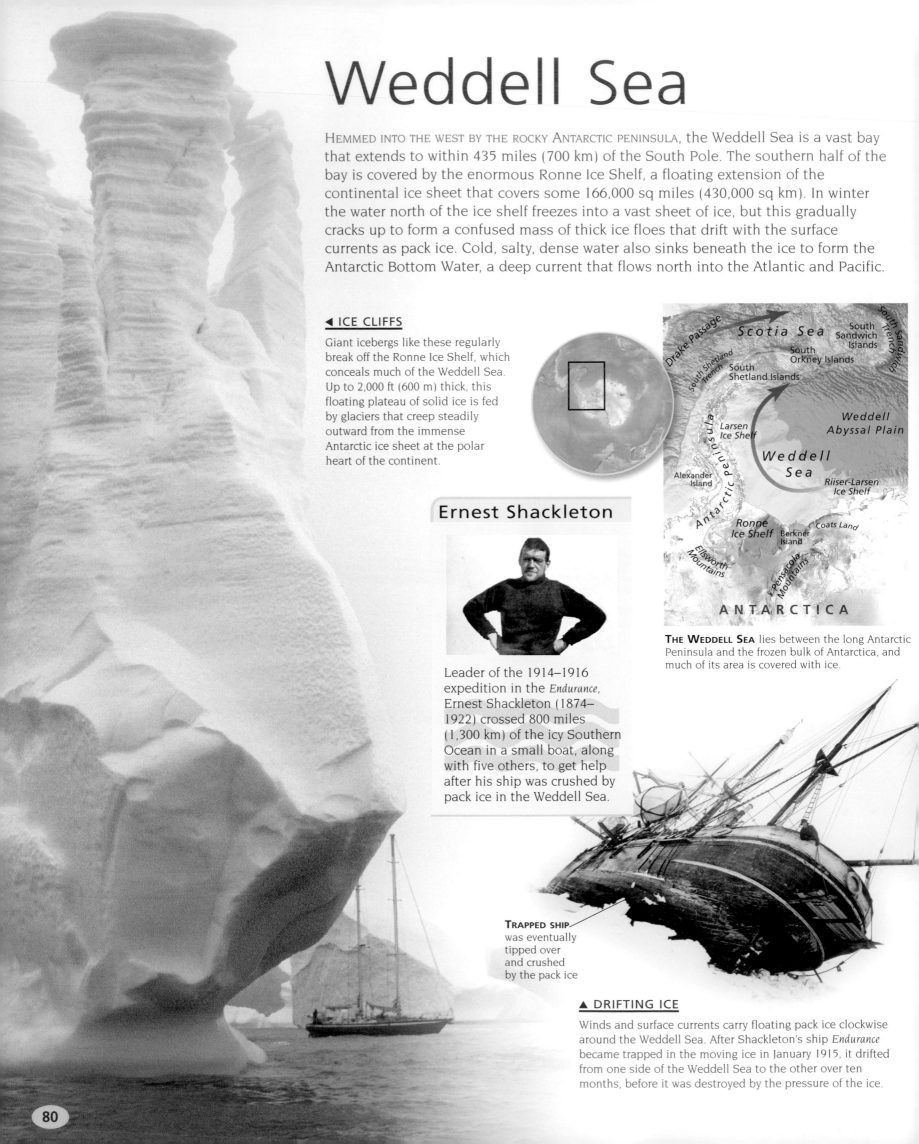

Weddell Sea

HEMMED INTO THE WEST BY THE ROCKY ANTARCTIC PENINSULA, the Weddell Sea is a vast bay that extends to within 435 miles (700 km) of the South Pole. The southern half of the bay is covered by the enormous Ronne Ice Shelf, a floating extension of the continental ice sheet that covers some 166,000 sq miles (430,000 sq km). In winter the water north of the ice shelf freezes into a vast sheet of ice, but this gradually cracks up to form a confused mass of thick ice floes that drift with the surface currents as pack ice. Cold, salty, dense water also sinks beneath the ice to form the Antarctic Bottom Water, a deep current that flows north into the Atlantic and Pacific.

◀ ICE CLIFFS

Giant icebergs like these regularly break off the Ronne Ice Shelf, which conceals much of the Weddell Sea. Up to 2,000 ft (600 m) thick, this floating plateau of solid ice is fed by glaciers that creep steadily outward from the immense Antarctic ice sheet at the polar heart of the continent.

Ernest Shackleton

Leader of the 1914–1916 expedition in the *Endurance*, Ernest Shackleton (1874–1922) crossed 800 miles (1,300 km) of the icy Southern Ocean in a small boat, along with five others, to get help after his ship was crushed by pack ice in the Weddell Sea.

THE WEDDELL SEA lies between the long Antarctic Peninsula and the frozen bulk of Antarctica, and much of its area is covered with ice.

TRAPPED SHIP was eventually tipped over and crushed by the pack ice

▲ DRIFTING ICE

Winds and surface currents carry floating pack ice clockwise around the Weddell Sea. After Shackleton's ship *Endurance* became trapped in the moving ice in January 1915, it drifted from one side of the Weddell Sea to the other over ten months, before it was destroyed by the pressure of the ice.

MALE EMPEROR takes charge of incubation, supporting the egg on his feet and keeping it warm under a fold of skin

WEDDELL SEAL may dive as deeply as 2,000 ft (600 m) to find prey, storing oxygen in its blood rather than its lungs

▲ ICY NURSERY

Most penguins breed on land, but emperor penguins breed on the sea ice of areas like the Weddell Sea. They incubate their eggs through the winter, huddling together for shelter from the freezing winds, so their chicks hatch in early spring. This gives the chicks as much time as possible to put on weight before summer ends.

HUNTING UNDER THE ICE ▶

In winter, most Antarctic animals head north to feed in open water as the sea ice expands away from the continent. But deep-diving Weddell seals stay behind to hunt fish and squid beneath the ice. They make breathing holes by using their teeth to enlarge existing fissures between ice floes, but as a result many Weddell seals suffer from worn teeth and other dental problems.

◀ POLAR MELTDOWN

Climate change is making the polar regions heat up faster than anywhere else on Earth. Summers on the Antarctic Peninsula are 3.6°F (2°C) warmer than they were in the 1960s, and this has probably led to the collapse of parts of the 820-ft (250-m) thick Larsen Ice Shelf on the western side of the Weddell Sea. These satellite images show how the ice has melted and broken up since 1993.

1993 The ice shelf filled three big bays on the eastern side of the Antarctic Peninsula—this shows the two northern bays

1995 In January the Larsen A Ice Shelf in the northern bay broke up, and Larsen B to the south was also shrinking

2000 Five years later, Larsen B had melted back to expose a rocky headland that had been icebound for thousands of years

2002 In just 35 days in February and March, 1,254 sq miles (3,250 sq km) of Larsen B broke up and drifted away

The Icy Ocean

IN WINTER THE SURFACE OF THE SOUTHERN OCEAN begins to freeze near the shores of Antarctica, and the ice extends north to cover up to 8 million sq miles (22 million sq km)—more than twice the area of Antarctica. In summer most of it melts away, leaving 1.5 million sq miles (4 million sq km) of permanent ice around the continent. Most of the wildlife follows the expanding ice edge away from the coast in winter, returning in summer to feast on the krill that multiply in the sunlit waters.

▲ TABULAR ICEBERG

Colossal flat-topped icebergs regularly break off the Antarctic ice shelves and drift into the Southern Ocean. In March 2000 an iceberg the size of Connecticut split from the Ross Ice Shelf—one of the biggest ever recorded.

THE OUTER LIMIT OF THE SOUTHERN OCEAN is marked by the Antarctic Convergence, where the ocean water suddenly becomes warmer

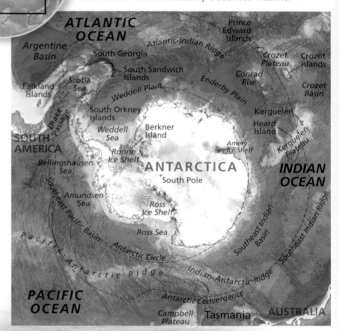

◄ PACK ICE

Bitterly cold air makes water at the ocean surface freeze into ice crystals, and these then congeal into soupy "grease ice." Further cooling forms thin plates of pancake ice that may freeze into a thicker, continuous sheet. But the swell usually breaks the sheet into a mosaic of ice floes, known as pack ice. The floes may then get driven together by winds and currents to form a confused but fairly stable sheet, as seen here.

LEOPARD SEAL makes short work of an Adelie penguin that it has seized beneath the ice

ICE FISH ►

Salty seawater freezes at 29°F (−1.8°C), so Antarctic waters are often colder than the usual freezing point of body fluids. Fish such as the ice fish survive because their blood contains natural antifreezes, which prevent the growth of deadly ice crystals.

AMBUSH KILLER ►

Millions of crabeater seals and Adelie penguins spend the winter on the pack ice, feeding on krill in nearby open water. But many fall victim to the leopard seal, a fearsome hunter that lurks in the water below the ice edge and ambushes young, inexperienced seals and penguins as they dive into the sea.

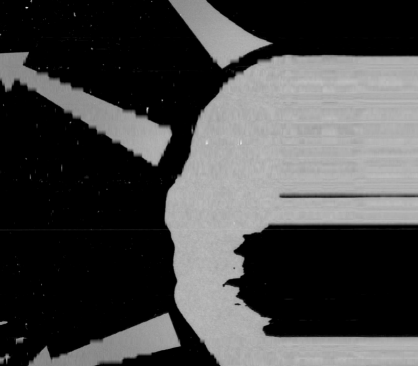

◄ KRILL SWARMS

When the winter ice breaks up in spring, phytoplankton in the water multiply to form a great "bloom." This provides food for vast swarms of shrimplike krill, which can turn the ocean surface red. These krill are the main prey of crabeater seals, many penguins, and the great whales that feed in Antarctic waters throughout the summer.

◄ GIANT WHALES

A blue whale takes huge mouthfuls of krill and water and uses its tongue to force the water out through the bristly baleen plates fringing its mouth. A single whale can eat 6 million krill a day like this and will feed every day for six months until the ocean starts freezing over. Then the whales migrate north to warm tropical waters, where the females give birth to their calves.

AFRICA

BLUE WHALE MIGRATION

The overlay shows how the sea ice expands in winter to cover most of the Southern Ocean, and how the blue whales that feed around Antarctica migrate north to warmer waters to breed.

SOUTH AMERICA

ANTARCTICA

INDIAN OCEAN

SUMMER THAW

Lifting the overlay reveals the whales feeding on the krill swarms that live around Antarctica in summer.

PACIFIC OCEAN

AUSTRALIA

KEY

▣	SUMMER SEA ICE
▢	WINTER SEA ICE
✈	BLUE WHALES
←	MIGRATION ROUTE

Ocean Facts

ALTHOUGH OCEANS COVER MOST OF THE PLANET, we still know surprisingly little about them. For the first ocean explorers, the seas simply offered a way of getting to distant continents and islands, but in the process they discovered a lot about ocean currents and wind systems. More recently we have begun to explore the ocean depths and the creatures that live in them and have discovered how the geology of the ocean floor has reshaped the Earth. Much of this research has been driven by a desire to exploit the sea's resources, from the fish in its waters to the oil beneath its rocky floor. Yet the more we find out, the more we realize that the health of the oceans is vital to our future—and to the future of all life.

Ocean Pioneers

THE EARLIEST OCEAN EXPLORERS left no records of their exploits. But there is evidence that people migrated to Indonesia by sea some 700,000 years ago, and to Australia around 50,000 years ago. About 2,000 years ago the Polynesians were crossing the Pacific, and 1,000 years later the Vikings had explored the north Atlantic as far as Newfoundland. But the great age of ocean exploration began with the epic voyages of Ferdinand Magellan and Francis Drake, and continued with the expeditions led by scientific pioneers such as Captain James Cook.

◀ VIKING NAVIGATORS

The Viking sagas tell of navigators like Eric the Red, who headed out across the Atlantic from Scandinavia to colonize Iceland and the southern tip of Greenland. They found their way across the stormy north Atlantic by using the altitude of the Sun and stars above the horizon to gauge their latitude, but they had no accurate way of knowing how far they had sailed.

SLEEK LONGSHIPS of Viking raiders resembled the bigger ships used for long voyages

▲ POLYNESIAN SETTLERS

The Polynesians began settling the islands of the South Pacific about 3,500 years ago. They developed ocean-going double canoes big enough to carry all their supplies, and a navigation system based on wave patterns and the stars. By 1000 CE they had spread across the Pacific to colonize Hawaii in the north, Easter Island in the southeast, and New Zealand in the southwest.

HUGE WAVES and storm-force winds make the Southern Ocean the most taxing part of any round-the-world race

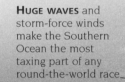

AROUND THE WORLD ▶

Little more than a pirate, Francis Drake sailed around Cape Horn into the Pacific in 1579 with the goal of attacking Spanish ports and treasure ships. He made a fortune, but became so notorious that he could not risk going back the same way. He was forced to sail on across the Pacific—and his ship, the *Golden Hind*, became the second to sail around the world after Magellan's.

RADAR SCANNER detects icebergs and other ships in darkness and fog

MAPPING THE OCEANS ▶

By the late 1700s navigation was a more exact science, enabling voyagers to map the oceans rather than just cross them. These explorers included Captain James Cook, who made three voyages to the Pacific, charting many of its coral islands and the coast of eastern Australia.

UNDER THE ICE ▶

By the 19th century, the only oceans left unexplored were those of the extreme north and south. By degrees the coasts of Antarctica were charted, and it became clear that there was no land beneath the polar ice of the Arctic. This was finally proved in 1958, when the nuclear submarine USS *Nautilus* passed under the ice at the North Pole.

▼ RACING ACROSS THE OCEANS

Today people regularly cross oceans in quite small boats, and even take part in non-top round-the-world sailing races. Accurate charts and advanced technology make these voyages much less dangerous than in the past. But the ocean has lost none of its destructive power, and it is still a risky, exhausting business.

Scientific Exploration

ONCE THE OCEANS HAD BEEN MAPPED, and the depths of shallow seas charted, the next challenge was to explore their nature. The science of oceanography was born in the 1870s, with the global oceanographic expeditions of the research ship H.M.S. *Challenger*. Its scientists investigated the deep oceans by dredging and sounding their depths from the surface. Such work is still undertaken, but modern submersibles now allow people to visit the deep ocean in person. Despite this, only a tiny fraction of the ocean floors has actually been explored, and these areas remain the most mysterious on Earth.

◀ THE CHALLENGER VOYAGE

Starting in 1872, H.M.S. *Challenger* sailed a four-year zigzag course of nearly 69,000 miles (111,000 km) across the world's oceans. During the voyage, the scientists on board collected hundreds of samples of the ocean floor and ocean water, and some 13,000 species of marine organisms. The ship also carried 144 miles (232 km) of sounding line to measure ocean depths. This revealed the existence of both the Mid-Atlantic Ridge and the Mariana Trench—although the scientists did not realize their geological significance at the time.

SCUBA DIVERS can swim freely, carrying their own air supply

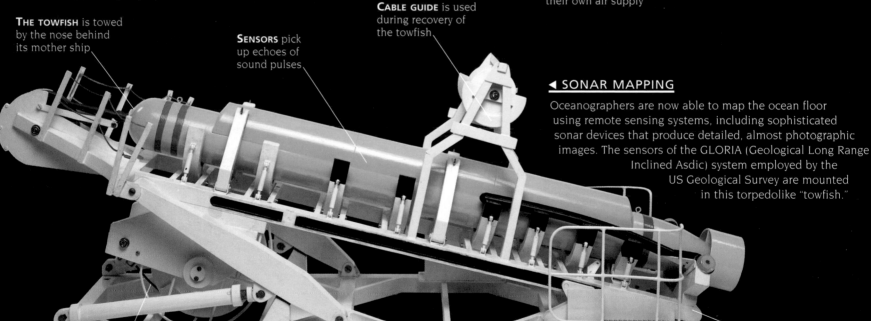

THE TOWFISH is towed by the nose behind its mother ship

SENSORS pick up echoes of sound pulses

CABLE GUIDE is used during recovery of the towfish

◀ SONAR MAPPING

Oceanographers are now able to map the ocean floor using remote sensing systems, including sophisticated sonar devices that produce detailed, almost photographic images. The sensors of the GLORIA (Geological Long Range Inclined Asdic) system employed by the US Geological Survey are mounted in this torpedolike "towfish."

LAUNCHING CRADLE is mounted on the back of the mother ship

ARMORED CABLE carries data to computers on the mother ship

HARD-HAT DIVER ▶

Exploring underwater in person was very dangerous before a reliable diving outfit was invented in the 1830s. This had a watertight suit, sealed to a metal helmet supplied with air from the surface. The diver could work underwater at depths of about 200 ft (60 m), but the suit was cumbersome and the restricted view from the helmet made it unsuitable for most scientific work.

SMALL GLASS WINDOWS in the metal helmet gave a view straight ahead and on each side, but looking up or down was difficult

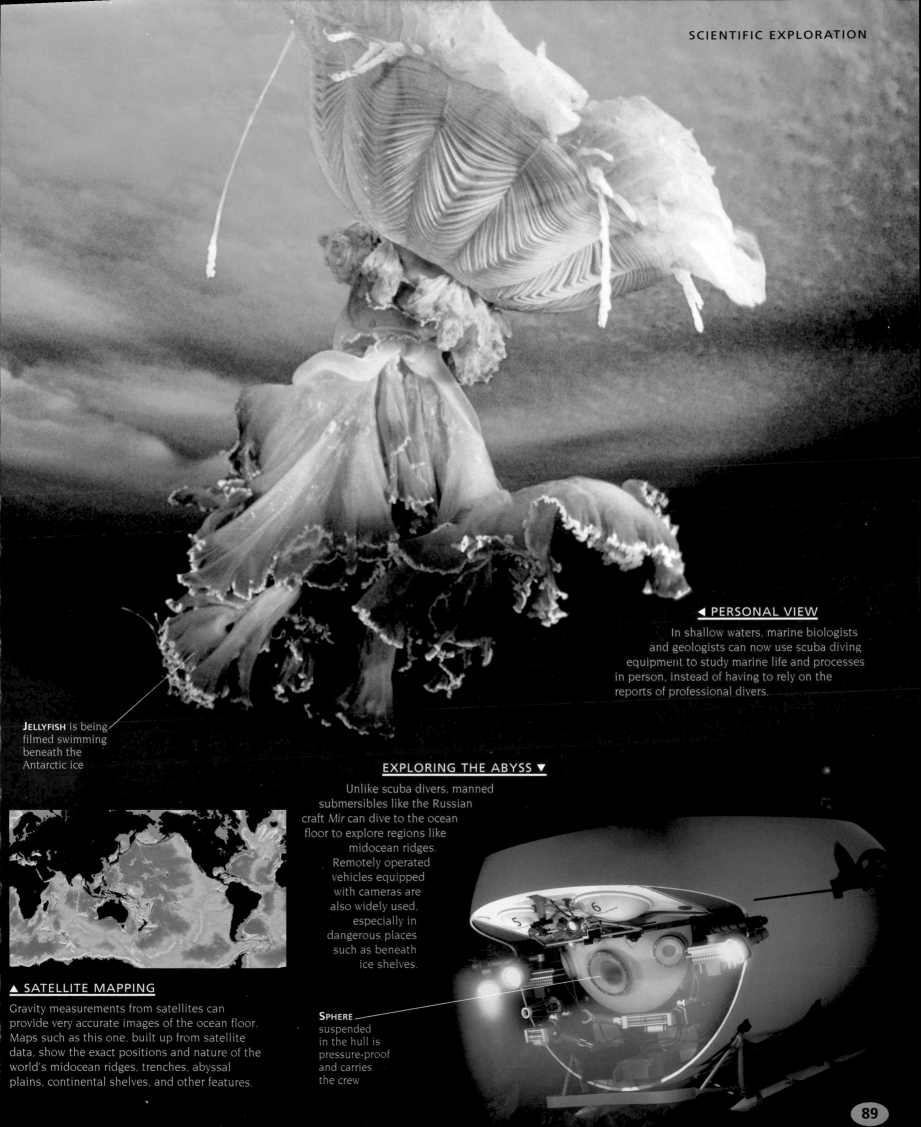

◀ **PERSONAL VIEW**

In shallow waters, marine biologists and geologists can now use scuba diving equipment to study marine life and processes in person, instead of having to rely on the reports of professional divers.

JELLYFISH is being filmed swimming beneath the Antarctic ice

EXPLORING THE ABYSS ▼

Unlike scuba divers, manned submersibles like the Russian craft *Mir* can dive to the ocean floor to explore regions like midocean ridges. Remotely operated vehicles equipped with cameras are also widely used, especially in dangerous places such as beneath ice shelves.

▲ **SATELLITE MAPPING**

Gravity measurements from satellites can provide very accurate images of the ocean floor. Maps such as this one, built up from satellite data, show the exact positions and nature of the world's midocean ridges, trenches, abyssal plains, continental shelves, and other features.

SPHERE suspended in the hull is pressure-proof and carries the crew

Exploiting the Oceans

FOR CENTURIES, PEOPLE HAVE BEEN FISHING THE OCEANS and traveling across them in ships. The seas have also been harvested for a wonderful variety of products, including salt, natural sponges, sharkskin leather, pearls, and even the purple dye that was once extracted from certain sea snails. More recently, the ocean has become an important source of oil, natural gas, and minerals. In dry countries, desalination plants remove the salt from seawater so it can be used for drinking water and irrigation. Yet one of the ocean's most valuable assets is its sheer beauty, which attracts tourists by the million to many coastal and island resorts.

▶ TRADING ROUTES

The sea has been used to transport trade goods since prehistoric times. At first the traders stayed close to the coasts, but as their ships became more seaworthy and navigation improved, they started crossing oceans. Today, lighter goods are carried by air, but ships are still the most efficient means of transporting heavy bulk goods like oil and minerals, and many ports are still important trading centers.

▲ FISHING

Fish and shellfish are eaten all over the world, and small boats like these are still used for local, low-intensity fishing in many coastal regions. But as human populations have grown, fishing has become big business. Large fleets of powerful ships now work far out on the deep oceans, using high-tech systems to locate fish shoals and scoop them out of the sea. The fish are then processed and packed on board, and frozen to keep them fresh.

▲ TOURISM

For many people, a tropical palm-fringed beach is the nearest thing to paradise, and they pay well to enjoy the experience. Since the expansion of air travel, tourism has become a major industry on many once remote islands, like those of the Maldives and Hawaii. For many, tourism has become the main source of income.

▶ MINERALS FROM THE SEA

About a third of the world's known reserves of oil and gas occur beneath coastal seas. Extracting them is difficult, dangerous, and expensive, but their high value makes it worthwhile. Sand and gravel are also dredged from the seabed, and there are plans to harvest more valuable minerals from the deep ocean floors, such as these metal-rich manganese nodules.

▼ SEA SALT

Seawater contains a lot of dissolved minerals, but the most abundant is sodium chloride, or common salt. It can be harvested from the sea by simply flooding shallow salt pans, and allowing the water to evaporate and leave the salt behind. This technique has been practised for centuries and still supplies roughly a third of the world's salt.

▲ FISH FARMING

Fishing relies on wild fish being able to breed faster than they are caught. The breeding rate of some sea fish can be greatly increased by farming them in submerged cages, like these Scottish salmon. This eases the pressure on wild fish, but it can cause pollution problems.

WHITE SALT CRYSTALS fringe this salt pan in Sri Lanka as seawater evaporates under the tropical sun

Ocean Conservation

THERE ARE NOW AT LEAST 6.5 BILLION PEOPLE living on the planet. We use so many of the world's resources, and cause so much pollution, that the health of the oceans is in serious danger. Many populations of sea fish have been wiped out by overfishing, and some species may soon be extinct. Other forms of marine life are being poisoned by chemicals and oil in the water, trapped in fishing gear, or killed by garbage dumped at sea. Coastal habitats are being destroyed, and coral reefs are dying as ocean waters warm up through climate change. We need to stop and try to reverse the damage before it is too late.

◄ OVERFISHING

Every year more than 83 million tons (75 million metric tons) of fish and shellfish are caught in the world's oceans. Industrial fishing is now so efficient that an entire shoal can be caught in a single net, eliminating a whole local population. Eventually the fish disappear. Once-rich fisheries like the North Sea and the Grand Banks have been virtually fished out in this way, and only tight restrictions are preventing some fish species from becoming globally extinct.

▲ DEADLY TRAPS

In the Southern Ocean, up to 100,000 albatrosses and other seabirds are killed every year by "longlines," which carry thousands of baited hooks. The birds try to snatch the bait as the lines are fed out, but get hooked and dragged underwater. Other air-breathing animals such dolphins, seals, and turtles often get caught in fishing nets and drown before they can be released. There are laws designed to prevent this, but many fishing fleets ignore them.

AN ENTIRE SHOAL of herring is caught by a purse seine net, which is laid around the fish and then closed off at the bottom

► POLLUTION

Every few years a big oil spill hits the news headlines, but most marine pollution is less dramatic, though just as harmful. Many coastal regions suffer from mudflows that silt up the water, and also from water pollution caused by sewage and fertilizers. Beaches all over the world are strewn with garbage, which can be deadly to animals that either eat it by accident or become trapped by it.

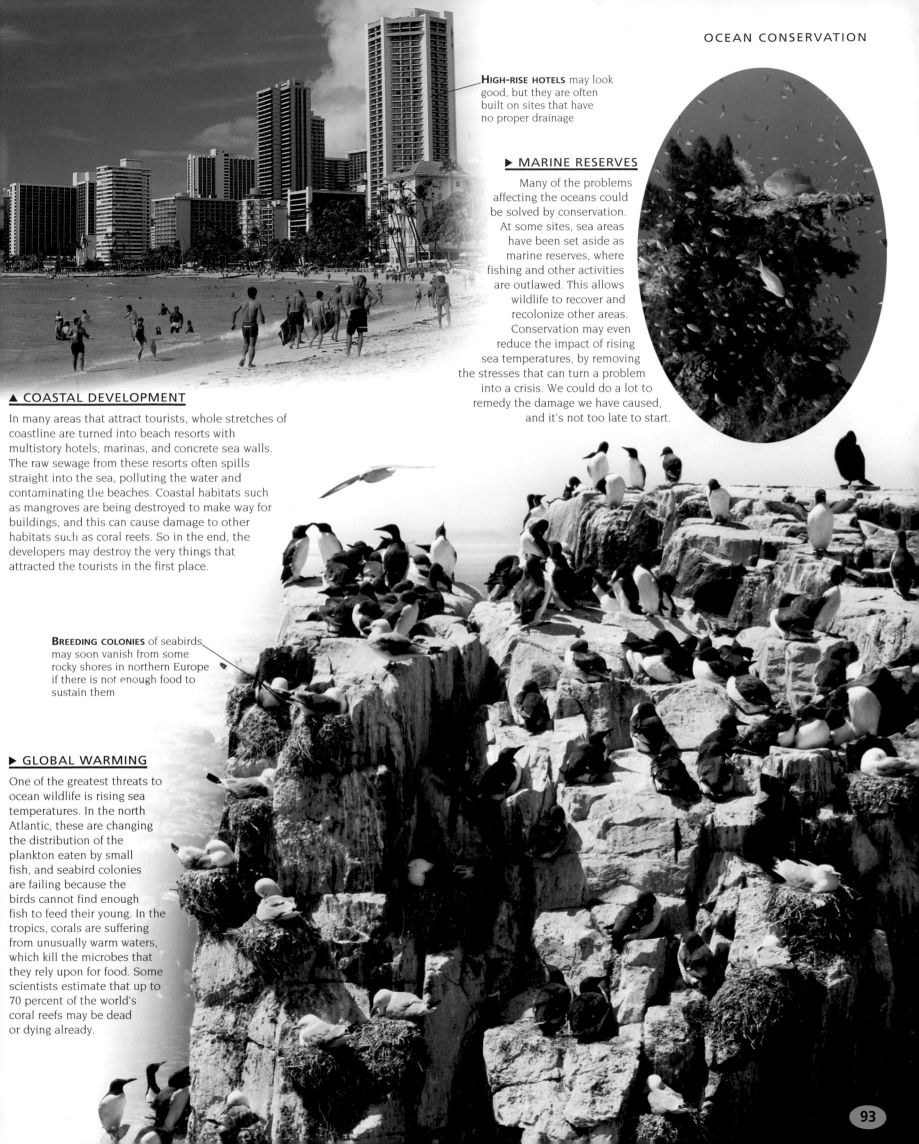

HIGH-RISE HOTELS may look good, but they are often built on sites that have no proper drainage

▶ MARINE RESERVES

Many of the problems affecting the oceans could be solved by conservation. At some sites, sea areas have been set aside as marine reserves, where fishing and other activities are outlawed. This allows wildlife to recover and recolonize other areas. Conservation may even reduce the impact of rising sea temperatures, by removing the stresses that can turn a problem into a crisis. We could do a lot to remedy the damage we have caused, and it's not too late to start.

▲ COASTAL DEVELOPMENT

In many areas that attract tourists, whole stretches of coastline are turned into beach resorts with multistory hotels, marinas, and concrete sea walls. The raw sewage from these resorts often spills straight into the sea, polluting the water and contaminating the beaches. Coastal habitats such as mangroves are being destroyed to make way for buildings, and this can cause damage to other habitats such as coral reefs. So in the end, the developers may destroy the very things that attracted the tourists in the first place.

BREEDING COLONIES of seabirds may soon vanish from some rocky shores in northern Europe if there is not enough food to sustain them

▶ GLOBAL WARMING

One of the greatest threats to ocean wildlife is rising sea temperatures. In the north Atlantic, these are changing the distribution of the plankton eaten by small fish, and seabird colonies are failing because the birds cannot find enough fish to feed their young. In the tropics, corals are suffering from unusually warm waters, which kill the microbes that they rely upon for food. Some scientists estimate that up to 70 percent of the world's coral reefs may be dead or dying already.

Glossary

ABYSSAL PLAIN
A flat area on the floor of the deep ocean, beyond the continental shelf, at a depth of about 13,000–20,000 ft (4,000–6,000 m).

ATOLL
A ring-shaped island formed from a coral reef based on a sunken extinct volcano.

BACKWASH
Movement of seawater down a beach after a wave has broken.

BARRIER REEF
A coral reef that protects a shallow lagoon from the deep ocean.

BASALT
A dark, heavy volcanic rock that forms oceanic crust, and erupts as molten lava from midocean ridges and hotspot volcanoes.

BEDROCK
The solid rock that lies beneath more recent, softer material or sediments.

BLACK SMOKER
A hot spring or hydrothermal vent on the ocean floor, usually at a midocean ridge, that erupts dark, cloudy, mineral-rich water.

CONTINENTAL SHELF
The submerged fringe of a continent, which lies beneath a shallow coastal sea.

CONTINENTAL SLOPE
The edge of the continental shelf, which slopes down to the ocean floor.

CONVERGENT BOUNDARY
A boundary between two plates of the Earth's crust that are moving together, marked by earthquakes and volcanoes.

CRUSTACEAN
An animal with a hard, shell-like external skeleton and paired, jointed legs, such as a crab or shrimp.

CURRENT
A flow of ocean water, driven by the wind or by differences in water density caused by temperature and/or salt content.

CYCLONE
A weather system marked by clouds, rain, and strong winds caused by air swirling into a region of rising warm, moist air.

DELTA
A fan of sand and silt laid down at the mouth of a river, usually with several river channels flowing over it.

DESALINATION
Removing the salt from seawater so it can be used for drinking or crop irrigation.

DIVERGENT BOUNDARY
A boundary between two plates of the Earth's crust that are moving apart.

DOLDRUMS
The oceanic region near the equator where there is normally little or no wind.

DYKE
A barrier designed to keep out the sea. Also a vertical sheet of volcanic rock.

EL NIÑO
A change in the ocean currents of the equatorial Pacific, when warm surface water moves east to suppress the normal flow of colder water. This affects the oceanic food supply and weather.

FILTER FEEDER
An animal that filters the water for food.

FISSURE
A broad crack, usually in rock.

FRACTURE ZONE
An area of extensive oceanic transform faults—sliding breaks in the ocean crust that separate different segments of a midocean ridge.

FRINGING REEF
A coral reef that surrounds a rocky, often volcanic island, and does not enclose a well-developed shallow lagoon.

GEOTHERMAL ENERGY
Energy for power generation obtained from hot rock, usually in a volcanically active region such as Iceland, or from drilling deep into the Earth.

GEYSER
A jet of hot water and steam that regularly erupts from volcanically heated rocks.

GLACIER
A mass of ice that is flowing very slowly downhill, usually through a deep valley.

GUANO
Thick deposits of seabird (or sometimes bat) droppings found where they nest.

GULF STREAM
The warm surface current that flows northeast across the Atlantic from near the Gulf of Mexico, carrying warm water toward Europe.

GYRE
A large-scale circular pattern of ocean currents, rotating clockwise north of the equator, and counterclockwise south of the equator.

HEADLAND
A narrow area of coastal land projecting between two bays.

HOTSPOT
An unusually hot part of the Earth's thick mantle, which makes volcanoes erupt through the crust above.

ISLAND ARC
A line of islands marking a boundary between two plates of the Earth's crust, created by volcanic activity as one plate plunges beneath the other and is destroyed.

JURASSIC
A period from 200 to 142 million years ago that formed part of the Mesozoic Era, or the age of the dinosaurs.

LAGOON
An area of shallow water that has been cut off from the sea.

LANDLOCKED
An area of water (or land) surrounded by land.

LATITUDE
An imaginary line marking a particular distance north or south from the equator.

LEAD
In the polar regions, a broad crack in sea ice that acts as a channel of open water.

LONGSHORE DRIFT
The movement of beach material along the shore by waves.

MANGROVE
A type of tree that grows in tidal water in the tropics, or a forest of these trees.

MANTLE
The thick layer of the Earth's interior between the crust and core, made of hot, partially molten rock.

MELTWATER
Water that flows off melting ice.

MIDOCEAN RIDGE
A ridge of submarine mountains on the ocean floor, created by a spreading rift between two plates of the Earth's crust.

MONSOON
A seasonal wind change that alters the weather pattern, especially in southern Asia.

MOTU
A low, sandy island on a coral reef.

MUDFLAT
A bank of fine mud that forms in sheltered water, and is exposed at low tide.

NUTRIENTS
Substances that living things need to build their body tissues.

PASSIVE BOUNDARY
A boundary between a continent and the ocean floor where there is no relative movement and no earthquake activity.

PERMAFROST
Permanently frozen ground.

PHOTOSYNTHESIS
The process by which green plants and some other organisms use the energy of light to make food from carbon dioxide gas and water.

PHYTOPLANKTON
Microscopic organisms that drift near the ocean surface and make food by photosynthesis.

PILLOW LAVA
Pillow-shaped lumps of volcanic rock, usually basalt, formed by lava erupting underwater and solidifying in the cold water.

PLANKTON
Living things that mainly drift in the water, rather than swimming actively.

PLANKTON BLOOM
An increase in the amount of plankton in water, caused by the organisms multiplying rapidly.

POLYNA
A broad area of open water in a polar ocean that is surrounded by sea ice.

PREVAILING WIND
A wind that blows from a particular direction most of the time.

RADAR
A system that uses pulses of radio waves to detect solid objects.

REEF
A ridge of submerged rock, often created by marine animals called corals.

RIFT
A break in the Earth's crust caused by the rocks moving apart.

SCUBA
An air-supply system used by divers. The word SCUBA stands for Self-Contained Underwater Breathing Apparatus.

SEAMOUNT
An ocean-floor volcano, active or extinct, that does not break the ocean surface to form an island.

SEDIMENT
Solid particles such as sand, silt, or mud, that have settled on the seabed or elsewhere. They may compact and harden to form sedimentary rock.

SONAR
A system that uses pulses of sound waves to detect solid objects.

SPIT
A sand or shingle beach that projects from the land and has water on both sides.

STORM SURGE
A local, temporary rise in sea level caused by storm winds and low air pressure.

SUBDUCTION ZONE
A boundary between two plates of the Earth's crust, where one plate plunges beneath the other and is destroyed.

SUBMERSIBLE
A craft designed to dive to the ocean depths.

SUBTROPICS
The regions immediately north of the Tropic of Cancer and south of the Tropic of Capricorn.

SUNLIT ZONE
The region of the ocean near the surface, where there is enough sunlight for phytoplankton and seaweeds to make food and grow.

THERMOHALINE CIRCULATION
A global flow of ocean currents, driven by variations in water density caused by differences of temperature and salt content.

TRADE WINDS
Steady winds that blow from certain directions in the tropical oceans.

TRENCH
In oceanography, a deep chasm in the ocean floor created by one plate of the Earth's crust being dragged beneath another.

TROPICS
The regions that lie between the Tropic of Cancer and the Tropic of Capricorn, including the equatorial zone.

TSUNAMI
A large wave produced by a submarine earthquake or landslide, or a volcanic eruption.

TUNDRA
Cold, treeless land that lies on the fringes of polar ice sheets, which freezes in winter and partially thaws out in summer.

TWILIGHT ZONE
The deep region of the ocean where only faint blue light penetrates from the surface.

UPWELLING ZONE
A part of the ocean where deep water rich in plant nutrients is drawn up to the surface.

ZOOPLANKTON
The community of mostly small animals that drift in the ocean, mainly near the surface.

ZOOXANTHELLAE
Microscopic organisms that live in the tissues of coral and other marine animals, and make food by photosynthesis.

Index

A

abyssal plains 23
Alaska, Gulf of 61, 70–71
Antarctica 76–83, 87
Arabian seas 52, 54–55
Arctic Ocean 24–31, 87
Atlantic Ocean 32–49
atolls, coral 67

B

Baltic Sea 39
beaches 16–17, 39
Bengal, Bay of 52, 56–57
Bering Sea 24
birds 92, 93
    Arctic Ocean 31
    Atlantic Ocean 37,
    38–39
    Pacific Ocean 66, 71,
    75
    Southern Ocean
    78–79, 81
Black Sea 33, 41
black smokers 72–73

C

Canadian Arctic
    24, 30–31
Caribbean 33, 44–45
Cavanaugh, Colleen 73
Challenger, H.M.S. 88
China Seas 60, 62–63
cliffs 16
climate change *see* global
    warming
coasts 16–17
Columbus, Christopher
    42
comb jellies 21
comets 8
conservation 92–93
continental shelves 5,
    16, 63

continents 4, 6, 7
Cook, Captain James 65,
    86, 87
coral islands 55, 66–67
coral reefs 19, 93
    Atlantic Ocean 45
    Great Barrier Reef 61,
    64–65
    Indian Ocean 54, 55
Cousteau, Jacques 40
crabs 58, 66
crocodiles 59
currents 10–11, 19
    Atlantic Ocean 34, 38, 42,
    44, 48
    Indian Ocean 52, 54
    Southern Ocean 77, 80

D, E

Darwin, Charles 67, 75
deep-sea life 22–23
deltas 46, 56
Doldrums 14
Drake, Francis 86, 87
earthquakes 6, 7, 57
East Pacific Rise 61,
    72–73
Easter Island 73
eels 42
explorers 86–89

F, G

fish
    Atlantic Ocean 43
    coral reefs 65, 66
    Indian Ocean 53
    Pacific Ocean 62–63, 70,
    74
    Southern Ocean 82
    in sunlit zone 20
    in twilight zone 22–23
fishing 34, 52, 90–91, 92
food chains 18–19, 20

Fundy, Bay of 35
Galápagos Islands 61, 74–75
geothermal energy 37
global warming 92, 93
    Antarctica 81
    Arctic Ocean 26, 27, 28
    coral reefs 65, 66
    Gulf of Mexico 46
Grand Banks 34
gravity 12
Great Barrier Reef 61, 64–65
guano 75
Gulf Stream 11, 38
gyres 10, 42, 43

H, I

Hawaii 61, 68–69
Heezen, Bruce 48
hot springs 23, 72–73
hurricanes 14, 15, 44, 46
hydrothermal vents 23,
    72–73
ice 11
    Arctic Ocean 24, 26–27
    ice floes 26, 80, 82
    ice shelves 80
    icebergs 31, 34, 35, 80, 82
    Southern Ocean 82–83
ice ages 38, 39
Iceland 36–37
Indian Ocean 40–49
Indonesia 57, 58–59
Inuit 31
islands
    Canadian Arctic islands
    24, 30–31
    coral islands 55, 66–67
    Indian Ocean 52
    island arcs 62, 70
    subantarctic islands 77,
    78–79
    volcanic 7, 36, 44, 58–59,
    62, 66–69, 70

K, L

krill 82, 83
Labrador Current 34

lava 4, 6, 62, 68
light, underwater 9, 20–21,
    22–23
longshore drift 17

M

Madagascar 52
Magellan, Ferdinand 59, 86
mangroves 17, 44, 56, 59
mantle 4, 6
Mariana Trench 62
Mediterranean 33, 40–41
Mexico, Gulf of 33, 46–47
Mid-Atlantic Ridge 33,
    36–37, 48
midocean ridges 6, 41,
    72–73
migration 10, 71, 83
minerals 91
monsoon 54, 56
Moon 12–13, 64
Mozambique Channel 51,
    52–53
mudflats 17

N, O

Nansen, Fridtjof 26
El Niño 74, 75
North Pole 26, 87
Northeast Atlantic 33, 38–39
Northwest Atlantic 33,
    34–35
ocean floor 4
ocean-floor spreading 6, 24,
    36, 72
ocean trenches 6, 7
Oceania 61, 66–67
oceanography 88
oil 29, 39, 46, 71, 91, 92

P, R

Pacific Ocean 4, 60–75
pack ice 26, 80, 82
Panama Canal 45
penguins 79, 81
Persian Gulf 55
phytoplankton 18–19, 20–21

Piccard, Jacques 63
plankton 18–19, 20–21,
    22–23, 41
polar bears 24, 26
polar seas 11
    Arctic Ocean 24–31
    Southern Ocean 76–83
pollution 40, 41, 46, 71, 92
Polynesians 86
predators 21, 22
rain 8, 69
Red Sea 54
reefs *see* coral reefs
rocks 4, 5, 16

S

salt 8, 91
salt marshes 17
sand, beaches 16–17
Sargasso Sea 33, 42, 43
scavengers 21, 22
scientific exploration 88–89
scuba diving 88–89
seals 26, 34, 41, 44, 79,
    81, 82
seaweeds 43, 71
sediments 5
Shackleton, Ernest 80
sharks 20, 21, 49, 62–63, 69
ships
    explorers 86–87
    icebreakers 29
    shipwrecks 35, 41, 63,
    78, 80
    slave ships 49
    trade 90
shore life 12
Siberian seas 24, 28–29
Southern Ocean 76–83
spices 58, 59
storms 14, 15, 56
subduction zones 6, 7,
    60, 62
submersibles 88, 89
Suez Canal 40, 55
Sunda Arc 52, 56, 58–59
sunlit zone 20–21

T

Tharp, Marie 48
tides 12–13
tourism 40, 79, 93
trade routes 90
tropical North Atlantic 33,
    42–43
tsunamis 56, 57
tubeworms 72–73
tundra 29
turtles 10, 45
twilight zone 22–23

U, V

upwelling zones 19, 48, 71
Vikings 34, 38, 86
volcanoes 6, 7, 8
    Caribbean 44
    Iceland 36–37
    Indonesia 58–59
    Mediterranean 40
    Pacific Ocean 62, 66–70

W

walruses 28
water 8–9
waves 14–15, 16
    rogue waves 53
    surfing 69
    tsunamis 56, 57
weather 8, 15
Weddell Sea 77, 80–81
West African seas 33,
    48–49
whales
    Arctic Ocean 26, 28, 31
    Atlantic Ocean 35, 49
    Indian Ocean 54–55
    Pacific Ocean 70–71
    Southern Ocean 83
Wilson, John Tuzo 68
winds 10, 14–15
    Indian Ocean 54

Z

Zheng He 56
zooplankton 18, 19, 20–23

Credits

The publisher would like to thank the following for their kind permission to reproduce their photographs: (abbreviations key: a-above, b-bottom, bg-background, c-center, f-far, l-left, r-right, t-top)

Alamy Images: A Room With Views 39b; Beaconstox 56tr; Dalgleish Images 42l; Andrew Darrington 33bl, 37cr; Dbimages 52c; Danita Delimont 7t, 45t; Robert Estall photo agency 34cr; John Ferro Sims 8tr; fstop2 38tl; Martin Harvey 52tl; David Hoskings 6–7b; ImageState 55cr; INTERFOTO Pressebildagentur 51cr, 58tl; Ladi Kirn 87c; LOOK Die Bildagentur der Fotografen GmbH 48 (bg); mediacolor's 24–25b, 30–31b; Natural Visions 43br; North Wind Picture Archives 35cr; Photo Network 8cl; Nicholas Pitt 39cr; Linda Reinink-Smith 13c; Rick & Nora Bowers 82cl; Royal Geographical Society 80br; Skyscan Photolibrary 17tr; Stephen Frink Collection 53tl; Visual&Written SL 30bl; **Ardea**: 90cr; Jean Paul Ferrero 64cl; Bob Gibbons 16br; Francois Gohier 12cl, 12clb, 18–19 (bg), 44bl, 61tr, 70b, 71cl; Chris Knights 38b; Ken Lucas 19cr; Pat Morris 20b; D. Parer & E. Parer-Cook 61crb, 75bl; Sid Roberts 35l; Douglas David Seifert 20t; M. Watson 61bc, 66c, 71bl; **The Art Archive**: Global Book Publishing 77c, 81t; **Bluegreen Pictures**: Rick Tomlinson 86–87b; Philip Stephen 14–15; **Cody Images**: 87tr; **Brandon Cole**: 92tr; **Corbis**: Yann Arthus-Bertrand 54cl; Bettmann 26cl, 40bl, 51tr, 56bc, 63cr, 71tr, 75cl; Jonathan Blair 33tr; British Petroleum/epa 33crb, 46b; Brandon D. Cole 21cr; Dean Conger 51b, 55tl; Jack Fields 34tl; Peter Guttman 24cl, 29bl; Rainer Hackenberg/zefa 41cr; Richard Hamilton Smith 11c; Wolfgang Kaehler 31cla; Vincent Laforet/Pool/Reuters 47tl; Jacques Langevin 55tr; Danny Lehman 45c; Amos Nachoum 69bl; NASA 47cl; David Pu'u 61br, 68–69, 84–85; Roger Ressmeyer 6cr; Jeffrey L. Rotman 33cla, 72bl; Kevin Schafer 61cra, 73tr; Alfio Scigliano/Sygma 40c; Paul A. Souders 4bl; Ralph White 23cl, 72cra, 73l; **DK Images**: Angus Oborn/Rough Guides 77t; Judith Miller/Wallis and Wallis 35tr; 22c, 22–23 (bg), 24t, 33cra, 59cl, 59cr, 65cr, 90–91t; Shaen Adey 16cr; Barnabas Kindersley 31cra; Martin Camm 26cr; Colin Sinclair 40–41; Courtesy of the National Maritime Museum, London 87tl; Ken Findlay 1cra, 33br; Francesca Yorke, Courtesy of the Royal Ontario Museum, Toronto 79tl; Michelle Grant 15tr; Frank Greenaway 19t, 20br, 21tr, 23b, 88c, 91cl; Helena Smith 90c; Nigel Hicks 19br; Zena Holloway 24–25 (bg), 29cra, 32 (bg), 35br, 43br, 45cl, 46hr, 50–51 (bg), 53cr, 55crb, 70br, 76 (bg), 79br (bg), 94–95, 96; Ian Cumming 66cl, 66ftr; Jaimie Marshall 74br; James Stevenson & Tina Chambers, Courtesy of the National Maritime Museum 86tr; Jane Miller 93br; Judith Miller/Roger Bradbury 63tr; David Peart 2–3, 20–21 (bg), 44t, 54c, 93tr; Ray Moller 88b; Rob Reichenfeld 93tl; Alex Robinson 17cl; Harry Taylor 49b, 83tl; Kim Taylor & Jane Burton 1clb, 22–23t, 56tc; Wilberforce Museum, Hull 49br; **Ecoscene**: Quentin Bates 92l; **exploretheabyss.com/Deep Sea Photography**: 21tl, 22bl, 22hr, 22cra, 22crb, 22fcra; David Batson 89br; **FLPA**: Norbert Wu/Minden Pictures 89t; NORBERT WU/Minden Pictures 81c; Tui De Roy/Minden Pictures 26c, 75t, 77b, 82t; Tom & Pam Gardner 59t; Michio Hoshino/Minden Pictures 28br; David Hoskings 30–31t, 78cl; S. Jonasson 33clb, 37tr; Gerard Lacz 34b; Frans Lanting/Minden Pictures 39tl, 58–59b, 80l; Chris Newbert/Minden Pictures 74l; Panda Photo 8br, 41tl; Gary K. Smith 5br; Rinie Van Muers/FotoNatura 26bc; **Getty Images**: Torsten Blackwood/AFP 66cr; Warren Bolster 51cl, 52–53b; Peter David 23cr; Iconica/Jeff Rotman 60br, 62–63; Lonely Planet Images/Jim Wark 47bl; Hans Strand 27tr; **Jim Green**: 36–37b, 37tl; **Jim Harrison**: 73cr; **Image Quest 3-D**: Masa Ushioda 49c; James D. Watt 65tr, 66b; **Kos Picture Source**: Bob Grieser 14b; Adam Wilson 86cl; **Courtesy of Lamont Doherty Earth Observatory**: 48br; William Haxby 72c; **Lee Gibbons**: Tin Moon 1crb, 9b; **Richard T. Lutz**: 73bc, 73clb; **Mary Evans Picture Library**: 88tl; **Ed Merritt/DK Images**: 1cla, 4tl, 7cla, 7clb, 11t, 12–13, 25, 27 (main), 27cl, 28ca, 28cr, 30cl, 30cla, 32, 34t, 34tr, 36cb, 36cr, 36t, 38cr, 38t, 40cr, 40t, 42cr, 42t, 43cl, 44cra, 44t, 46cal, 46tl, 47r, 48t, 48tr, 50, 52cr, 52t, 54tc, 54tr, 56cl, 56tl, 57r, 58cr, 58t, 60–61t, 62cr, 62t, 64tc, 64tr, 66cra, 66tr, 68c, 68ca, 68tr, 70tc, 70tr, 72tc, 72tl, 74c, 74cr, 76, 78tc, 78tr, 80ca, 80cr, 82ca, 82cr, 83b; **NASA**: 15cr, 18bl, 30c, 63tl; **National Geographic Image Collection**: Paul Nicklen 29cl; Brian J. Skerry 28cl; **naturepl.com**: Doug Allan 31c, 82br; Jeff Foott 71tl; Jurgen Freund 61bl, 64–65b, 65tl; Ben Osborne 28–29t; Peter Oxford 45bl; Doug Perrine 10b; Martin H. Smith 39tr; **NOAA**: 80c, 89bl, 91cr; **Ontario Science Centre**: 68br; **OSF**: Chris & Monique Fallows 49t; Rodger Jackman 12bc; Pacific Stock 43r; **PA Photos**: Miguel Gomez/AP 44cr; **Photoshot/NHPA**: ANT Photo Library 58c; B. & C. Alexander 26t, 29br; Georgette Douwma 65c; Trevor McDonald 21b; Taketomo Shiratori 73ca; **Science Photo Library**: Dee Breger 5cr; British Antarctic Survey 78c, 78–79b; Jim Corwin 16l; Geoeye 57bl, 57tl, 67b; W. Haxby, Lamont-Doherty Earth Observatory 5tr; Jan Hinsch 18c; R. B. Husar/NASA 75cr; Rudiger Lehnen 9tc; M-SAT LTD 39; Kenneth Murray 69br; Stephen & Donna O'Meara 44cl; Carleton Ray 41cl; Madeleine Redburn 17b; Alexis Rosenfeld 9tr, 41tr; Peter Scoones 53tr; US Geological Survey 62cl; Tom Van Sant, Geosphere Project Planetary Visions 4–5; Andrew G. Wood 43bc; **seapics.com**: Doc White 62c; Phillip Colla 83tr; **splashdowndirect.com**: Mike Nolan 54–55b; Mike Phimister 79tr; **Still Pictures**: Mark Carwardine 79c; Markus Dlouhy 13r; Peter Legler-Unep 92br; Mark Edwards 90–91b; Peter Schickert 8bl; Norbert Wu 83; **Visible Earth**: http://visibleearth.nasa.gov/ 56c, 70l; Jeff Schmaltz/ http://visibleearth.nasa.gov/33cr

Jacket images: Front: **Corbis**: Matthias Kulka (bg); Jeffrey L. Rotman fbr; Stuart Westmorland fbl; **DK Images**: Jerry Young cr (CD/striped fish); **Getty Images**: Visuals Unlimited cl; **Michelle Millar**: bl (whale). Back: **Corbis**: Jeffrey L. Rotman fbr; Stuart Westmorland fbl; **Michelle Millar**: bl (whale); **Science Photo Library**: Alexis Rosenfeld (bg). Spine: **Corbis**: Jean Guichard.

All other images © Dorling Kindersley
For further information see: www.dkimages.com

The publisher would also like to thank
Hazel Beynon, and Hilary Bird for the index.